Experience It!

PEARSON

Boston, Massachusetts
Chandler, Arizona
Glenview, Illinois
Upper Saddle River, New Jersey

Daniel M. Shea, author, *American Government: Experience It!*

After earning a Bachelor of Arts degree in Political Science from the State University of New York at Oswego, Daniel M. Shea received a Master of Arts in Campaign Management from the University of West Florida. He then worked as regional coordinator for the New York State Democratic Assembly Campaign Committee. He returned to graduate school and received a Ph.D. in Political Science from the State University of New York at Albany in 1993. Shea was named a research fellow at the Ray C. Bliss Institute of Applied Politics at the University of Akron in 1993, and in 1999, joined the faculty at Allegheny College where he was named Director of the Center for Political Participation in 2002. Shea's research and teaching specializations are campaigns and elections, political parties, legislative dynamics, politics of popular culture, and youth mobilization. He has written or edited some 12 books and dozens of articles, including the popular college text, *Living Democracy.*

ISBN 10: 0-13-365675-6
ISBN 13: 978-0-13-365675-6

4 5 6 7 8 9 10 11 V036 13 12 11

Table of Contents

Photo Credits

Text Acknowledgments

Table of Contents

• AMERICAN GOVERNMENT *ESSENTIAL QUESTIONS VIDEO* DVD AND ONLINE

Integrated videos introduce content and focus in on each unit's Essential Question. Students watch a combination of historical and contemporary footage and are presented with the unit Essential Question to allow them to begin thinking about how they might answer the Essential Question.

• *ESSENTIAL QUESTIONS JOURNAL*

This dynamic journal guides students in exploring the 🔃 Essential Questions in each unit.

• EXPERIENCE IT! *TEACHER'S GUIDE AND LESSON PLANNER*

The *Teacher's Guide and Lesson Planner* includes detailed daily lesson plans for teaching essential content through in-class and online interactivities. Each lesson plan references Background Notes on key topics, Activity Worksheets, and Assessments. Look for this symbol 🕐 in your *Teacher's Guide and Lesson Planner* to locate this wealth of online materials.

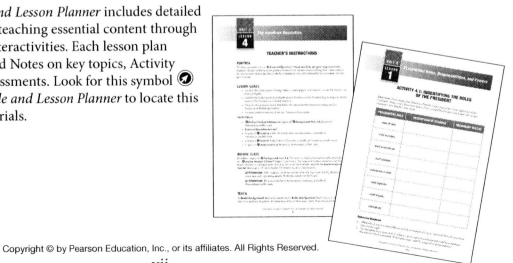

AMERICAN GOVERNMENT: EXPERIENCE IT!

This interactive program is designed to give you and your students an alternate approach to teaching and learning American Government through hands-on activities, simulations, and online decision-making interactivities, all centered around Essential Questions. Each unit of study includes a full set of step-by-step **Lesson Plans** that direct you to online **Background Notes, Activities,** and **Assessments,** as well as to the **American Government** *Essential Questions Video* and **Online Decision-Making Interactivities.** Each unit also includes a **Simulation Activity** in which students apply what they have learned throughout the unit and answer the unit Essential Question in their *Essential Questions Journal.*

EXPERIENCE IT! RESOURCES

• EXPERIENCE IT! ACTIVITY PACK

This dynamic activity pack includes folders for each of the seven units, housing full color, hands-on maps, posters, photos, charts, graphs, role cards, and primary source documents for students to use in the simulation activity for each unit.

• EXPERIENCE IT! ONLINE INTERACTIVE DECISION-MAKING ACTIVITIES

Each unit includes an interactive online decision-making game. Students plan a new government, help the President make energy policy, negotiate a trade agreement and much more. Students gain practice in making tough choices and learning what the consequences of those choices will be.

• TWO ONLINE STUDENT EDITIONS

Throughout the course, students access the trusted *Magruder's American Government* and the *American Government Foundations Series* textbooks.

• ONLINE TEACHER EDITIONS AND TEACHING RESOURCES

Use online access to *Magruder's American Government* and *Government Foundations Series* Teacher Editions for additional lesson plans and information as well as leveled Teaching Resources and assessments.

The Confirmation Process of a Presidential Appointee

President Nominates
- White House staff conducts search for candidate.
- Key experts provide White House with information and guidance.
- President selects nominee and submits choice to Senate.

Senate Committee Examines
- Nominee testifies before appropriate Senate committee.
- Majority vote required before nominee is recommended to Senate.

Senate Debates
- Full Senate considers the nomination.
- Senators debate the nominee's qualifications.
- If Senate strongly opposes, President may withdraw nomination or nominee may bow out.
- Floor vote is taken.

Nominee Confirmed
- A simple majority Senate vote approves nominee

Nominee Rejected*
- Nominee does not get a simple majority and is rejected. * Process begins again.*

© Pearson Education, Inc., or its affiliates. All rights reserved.

HOW TO USE YOUR *AMERICAN GOVERNMENT: EXPERIENCE IT!* RESOURCES

Each lesson plan in the *American Government: Experience It!* **Teacher's Guide and Lesson Planner** starts with Teacher Instructions that inform you of the purpose of the lesson, identify lesson goals, list materials needed for the lesson, give you suggestions for what students can do before class, and provide detailed steps for teaching the lesson. Online you will find a vast number of resources to supplement the lesson plan: Background Notes provide you and your students with a quick look at essential content, Activity Worksheets engage students with essential content, and Assessments allow you to gauge student understanding. At various points throughout the lesson, references to the **Online** *Magruder's American Government* **Student Edition** are provided for easy reference and additional information. Lesson plans also include instructions for using **Decision-Making Interactivities** to reinforce decision-making skills and the *Essential Questions Journal* to prepare students for answering each unit's Essential Question.

Each unit also contains detailed instructions for a multiple-day simulation activity in which students work in small groups and as a class to ultimately frame an answer to each unit's Essential Question. Students use the creatively designed materials—role cards, posters, maps, newspaper articles, and photographs—from the *American Government: Experience It!* **Activity Pack** to role-play and work through the activity. Additional source materials are available online, along with activities to guide students through each simulation.

Look for this symbol ❦ throughout the Lesson Plans for online resources available at PearsonSuccessNet.com

Foundations of American Government

UNIT OVERVIEW

This group of lessons focuses on the establishment of the Constitution and the American system of government. It includes exploration of landmark English documents, Enlightenment philosophers, the Declaration of Independence, and the debates of the Constitutional Convention. The lessons culminate in a reconstruction of those debates. At the end of this unit, students will craft an answer to the ❸ Essential Question: *What should be the goals of government?* You may wish to have students begin their study by completing the *Essential Questions Journal* Unit 1 Warmup, p. 2.

UNIT GOALS

- Understand the core functions of government.
- Examine influences on the development of the United States government.
- Analyze the Declaration of Independence, including its philosophical foundations and the grievances that established an argument for a new nation.
- Reconstruct the great debates that took place during the creation of the Constitution.
- Analyze the United States Constitution, including the amendments.

TIME ALLOTMENT

This unit of activities is intended to be taught in 13 days (or 7 days on a block schedule).

DAY 1	Lesson 1	Concepts of Government and the State
DAY 2	Lesson 2	Interactive Decision-Making: Creating a Government
DAY 3	Lesson 3	Foundations of American Rights and Government
DAY 4	Lesson 4	The American Revolution
DAY 5	Lesson 5	The Articles of Confederation
DAYS 6–9	Lesson 6	The Constitutional Convention
DAY 10	Lesson 7	Ratification of the Constitution
DAY 11	Lesson 8	The Six Principles of the Constitution
DAY 12	Lesson 9	Bill of Rights and Seventeen Other Amendments
DAY 13	Lesson 10	Wrap-Up

ENDURING UNDERSTANDINGS

- Government affects our daily lives in countless ways by maintaining civil society, safeguarding rights, and preventing anarchy.
- The chaos under the Articles of Confederation led to a more powerful central government.
- The Framers created a Constitution that addressed the major concerns of the states.
- The United States Constitution is based on six principles: popular sovereignty, limited government, separation of powers, checks and balances, judicial review, and federalism.
- Our government protects and guarantees individual freedom and security, private property, freedom of belief and expression, and fair and equal treatment before the law.

TEACHER INSTRUCTIONS

PURPOSE

To frame an answer to the 🌐 **Essential Question**: *What should be the goals of government?*, students need to understand reasons why governments are created and the various forms that governments can take.

LESSON GOALS

- Identify important activities of government by studying democracies and dictatorships.
- Discuss reasons for establishing government after researching four different governments.
- Discuss how prominently government figures into their lives.

MATERIALS

- 🔊 **Online Student Edition** and copies of 🔊 **Background Note 1.1,** located at PearsonSuccessNet.com
- *Essential Questions Journal*
- Copies of 🔊 **Activity 1.1,** Lord of the Flies *Excerpts* located at PearsonSuccessNet.com
- Internet access
- Copies of 🔊 **Assessment 1.1,** located at PearsonSuccessNet.com

BEFORE CLASS

Distribute copies of the 🔊 **Background Note 1.1.** For more in-depth information, refer students to the 🔊 **Online Student Edition** Chapter 1, Sections 1 and 2. You may wish to have students read these materials before coming to class. You may also want students to complete the *Essential Questions Journal* Warmup, p. 3, and Chapter 1 Exploration, p. 4, before class.

> **L2 Differentiate** Ask students to read 🔊 **Background Note 1.1** aloud and define the terms in boldface. Then have volunteers explain why these terms are important for understanding the Background Note.

> **L2 Differentiate** Have students listen to the online summary, available at PearsonSuccessNet.com.

TEACH

1. Activate Prior Knowledge Tell students that the goal of this unit is to explore the 🌐 **Essential Question**: *What should be the goals of government?* To help them start thinking about this question, have them take out the *Essential Questions Journal* Unit Warmup, p. 2, where they identified the most important activities of government, or have them complete the assignment in class. Survey students about which governmental activities they consider most important. Record their responses on the board. Discuss differences and similarities in student choices, and invite them to explain their choices. What category of activity appeared most often on students' lists? What factors—age, geography, political background, etc—might have affected student choices?

2. Introduce the Lesson Ask students to identify and define the two main types of government: democracy, where people hold the supreme power and government is carried out with their consent; and dictatorship, where rulers are not responsible to the will of the people. Pass out ⭕**Activity 1.1,** Lord of the Flies *Excerpts* and call on volunteers to read the introductions and excerpts. Ask students what form of government each scene represents. Encourage them to compare and contrast the two scenes and to speculate about Sir William Golding's ideas on government. To what extent do they agree or disagree?

3. Activity Divide the class into four groups, and give each group one of the following countries: United Kingdom, United States, Myanmar (Burma), or China. Tell them that they should research their country's government to understand how it came about, and how it is organized today. Their research should be based on the following criteria: the official name of the country, the form of government, the chief of state, the head of the government, the origins of the current government, and the way in which elections are held. This information can be found at the CIA World Factbook website (www.cia.gov/library/publications/the-world-factbook/).

4. Debrief Ask students to reflect as a class on the results of their research. Then ask how they would classify each of the four governments—as a democracy or a dictatorship. Based on their research, which form of government seems the most effective? At this time, students might also want to revisit the **Essential Questions Journal** Chapter 1 Warmup, p. 3, where they responded to a quote by Alexander Hamilton on the need for government and assessed the importance of government to themselves.

5. Assess Distribute ⭕**Assessment 1.1,** which asks students to identify three areas of their lives in which government plays a role and to evaluate its significance in these areas.

EXTEND THE LESSON

L3 Differentiate Have students watch *Lord of the Flies,* which is available in two versions: the 1963 film and the 1990 film. Ask them to write a paragraph concerning what the movie suggests about the goals of government.

L4 Differentiate Have students write an essay explaining whether they agree or disagree with Golding's ideas on government and human nature, and what the movie suggests to them about the goals of government. Encourage students to read the Nobel Laureate's book.

TEACHER INSTRUCTIONS

PURPOSE

To help students gain an understanding of how and why government is formed, what forms of government exist, and how it functions in various forms, students are presented with an online activity in which they must form a government after finding themselves on a deserted island.

LESSON GOALS

- Explain the basic functions of government.
- Compare and contrast various forms of government.

MATERIALS

- ⊘ **Online Interactive Decision-Making,** located at PearsonSuccessNet.com
- *Essentials Questions Journal*

BEFORE CLASS

Refer students to the ⊘ **Online Student Edition** Chapter 1, Sections 1 and 2. You may wish to have students read these materials before coming to class. You may also want students to complete the *Essential Questions Journal* Chapter 1 Warmup, p. 3, and Exploration pp. 4–6, before class.

TEACH

1. Introduce the Lesson Tell students that they will explore types of government, why they are formed, and their purpose. They will do this through an online simulation, in which they must form a government on a deserted island.

2. Complete the Activity Have students complete the online activity in class or assign the simulation as homework. NOTE: If you decide to give this as a homework assignment, conduct the Debrief at the beginning of class and then continue with the next day's lesson plan described on the following page.

3. Debrief Once students have completed the online simulation, lead a discussion about the necessity of government. Ask: **What could have happened when no formal government existed?** *(Students should understand that when this happens, anarchy and chaos occur, and it is possible for a dictatorship to form.)* Then, ask: **What kind of government worked best? Why?** *(Answers will vary, but students should understand that an organized government that tries to be fair to all is the best way to govern.)*

4. Assess Have students write 3–5 conclusions they can draw about the necessity of government from the online activity. You may wish to have students share these conclusions in class and follow up with a discussion of how the interactivity helps provide an answer to the ⊕ **Essential Question: *What should be the goals of government?*** You may also want to have students complete the Chapter 1 Essential Question Essay on p. 10 in their *Essential Questions Journal.*

TEACHER INSTRUCTIONS

PURPOSE

To frame an answer to the 💡 **Essential Question:** *What should be the goals of government?*, students should know the historical basis of American rights and government.

LESSON GOALS

- Analyze landmark English documents by reading selected excerpts.
- Identify the influences of Enlightenment thinkers by pointing out similar principles in the Constitution.
- Discuss the philosophical context of the Revolutionary War era by finding Enlightenment influences in the Framers' beliefs.

MATERIALS

- ⊘ **Online Student Edition** and copies of ⊘ **Background Note 1.3,** located at PearsonSuccessNet.com
- *Essential Questions Journal*
- Copies of ⊘ **Activity 1.3:** *Landmark English Documents,* located at PearsonSuccessNet.com
- Copies of ⊘ **Assessment 1.3,** located at PearsonSuccessNet.com

BEFORE CLASS

Distribute copies of ⊘ **Background Note 1.3.** For more in-depth information, refer students to the ⊘ **Online Student Edition** Chapter 2, Section 1. You may wish to have students read these materials before coming to class. You may also want students to complete the *Essential Questions Journal* Warmup, p. 11, and Chapter 2 Exploration, p. 12, before class.

> **L2 Differentiate** Help students create an outline of the Background Note by identifying the main idea in each philosopher's biography, as well as the supporting details. Write the outline on the board.

> **L2 Differentiate** Have students listen to the online summary, available at PearsonSuccessNet.com.

TEACH

1. Build Background Ask students to name the three major British documents on which many American government principles are based. Write the names of these documents on the board and list the major principles of each one. Ask students if they can think of any principles of United States democracy that sound similar.

2. Introduce the Lesson Ask students to name some basic rights and freedoms that are protected by the United States government. Ask: **In what countries do people enjoy these same rights? In**

what countries are citizens denied these rights? Ask students to consider what it would be like to live in a country where these rights are denied. Encourage students to explain where they think these rights originated. List their responses on the board in the first column of a two-column chart.

> **L2 Differentiate ELL** If you think they would be comfortable sharing, invite students who have lived in countries where rights are denied to talk about their experiences.

3. Complete the Activity Tell students that they will now review the landmark English documents. Explain that these documents established rights that were revolutionary in their day. Students will also learn about philosophers who influenced the founders of our nation. Distribute ⊘**Activity 1.3:** *Landmark English Documents,* and have students work in three groups. Assign each group one landmark document. Have group members study the document together to find passages that are reflected in their own government. Have them answer the three questions on the final page of the activity sheet. Then have groups read ⊘**Background Note 1.3** together and summarize each thinker's significance and influence. Ask students to name any similarities between the beliefs of the Enlightenment thinkers and the ideas put forth in the United States Constitution.

4. Debrief Call on a volunteer from each group to share answers to the questions about their document. Then discuss the Enlightenment thinkers and their importance in the development of our government and our basic rights. Return to the list from the Lesson 3 introduction and invite students to share how their views have changed on our rights and their origins. List their responses in the second column of the chart.

5. Assess Distribute ⊘**Assessment 1.3,** which asks students to identify three rights from the landmark documents that remain relevant today and to explain the significance of these rights in students' own lives.

EXTEND THE LESSON ▬▬▬▬▬▬

> **L3 Differentiate** Have small groups research the historical background of each of the three landmark documents. Ask groups to present the information in a newspaper article explaining the circumstances that drove English citizens to demand the protections secured in each document.

> **L2 Differentiate** Have students research to answer the following questions for each document: (1) Who was the ruler of England at the time the document was created?, (2) What actions did English citizens take to get the document signed?, and (3) Why did they demand this document be signed?

> **L4 Differentiate** Have students research and write a newspaper article on their own.

TEACHER'S INSTRUCTIONS

PURPOSE

To frame an answer to the 🌐 **Essential Question:** *What should be the goals of government?,* students should understand the political turmoil and revolutionary thinking that culminated in the Declaration of Independence, the Revolutionary War, and, ultimately, the formation of a new government.

LESSON GOALS

- Analyze the Declaration of Independence, paying particular attention to the Declaration of Natural Rights.
- Identify the influence of the Enlightenment thinkers on the Framers by pointing out similar ideas in the Declaration of Independence.
- Describe the political unrest that led to the American Revolution by citing specific instances of British oppression.
- Analyze political cartoons from the American Revolution.

MATERIALS

- 📀**Online Student Edition** and copies of 📀**Background Note 1.4,** located at PearsonSuccessNet.com
- *Essential Questions Journal*
- Copies of 📀**Activity 1.4A,** *The Declaration of Independence,* available at PearsonSuccessNet.com
- Copies of 📀**Activity 1.4B,** *Political Cartoons,* available at PearsonSuccessNet.com
- Copies of 📀**Assessment 1.4,** located at PearsonSuccessNet.com

BEFORE CLASS

Distribute copies of 📀**Background Note 1.4.** For more in-depth information, refer students to the 📀**Online Student Edition** Chapter 2, Section 2. You may wish to have students read these materials before coming to class. You may also want students to complete the *Essential Questions Journal* Warmup, p. 11, and Chapter 2 Exploration, p. 12, before class.

> **L2 Differentiate** Help students create an outline of the Background Note by identifying the main idea and supporting details. Write the outline on the board.

> **L2 Differentiate** Have students listen to the online summary, available at PearsonSuccessNet.com.

TEACH

1. Build Background Remind students of the **Reflection Question** from Lesson 3: *The American colonists fought the Revolutionary War for their basic rights. Does this lesson help you* *understand why?* Invite students to share their responses. Continue the discussion after a shared reading of ⊘ **Activity 1.4A:** *The Declaration of Independence.* Focus students' attention on the Declaration of Natural Rights and the list of grievances.

> **L2 Differentiate ELL** Write the following words on the board: *self-evident* (obvious); *endowed* (given); *inalienable* (not able to be taken away); *pursuit* (search); *instituted* (set up); *deriving* (getting); *consent* (permission); *destructive* (hurtful); *abolish* (to ban); *assent* (to agree); *relinquish* (to give up); *depository* (a place for safekeeping); *dissolution* (the act of breaking up); *annihilation* (destruction); *hither* (to this place); *jurisdiction* (authority); *quartering* (housing); *abdicated* (cast off); *perfidy* (disloyalty); *insurrections* (revolutions). Have volunteers define each word, or provide a definition for them; write each definition on the board.

2. Introduce the Lesson Explain that students will be studying some political cartoons from the Revolutionary War era and comparing them to passages in the Declaration of Independence. Ask students to discuss the kinds of information that political cartoons can convey. Then ask: **How could political cartoons better spread the messages Jefferson was writing in the Declaration of Independence?** *(By putting Jefferson's words into pictures, the messages became more accessible and more dramatic.)*

3. Complete the Activity Ask students to consider why cartoons became a potent propaganda tool before the War for Independence. Point out that the colonial cartoons convey some of the same messages found in the Declaration of Independence, while the British cartoons react to these messages.

Go over the various symbols in each cartoon. In Cartoon 1a, ask students what a skull-and-crossbones and the color black mean to them. In Cartoon 1b, tell students that a lion is a popular symbol for Great Britain, and show students an image of the original "Join or Die" cartoon. For Cartoon 2a, point out Treasury Secretary Grenville (fourth from left) holding the coffin. Ask, **Why do you think the cartoonist shows Grenville holding a coffin?** Point out the symbols of trade and industry in the background. For Cartoon 2b, remind students that colonists tarred and feathered British tax collectors, and that they dumped tea into Boston Harbor to protest the Tea Act. Ask, **What do you think the noose hanging from the Liberty Tree represents?**

Ask students to consider why these issues were so important to the colonists. Have students work in pairs for 20 minutes to answer the questions on ⊘ **Activity 1.4B,** *Political Cartoons.*

4. Debrief Invite volunteers to share their answers from the worksheet. Encourage them to reflect on the colonists' grievances and the British response to those grievances. Ask: **Which makes a greater impact on you, the words of the Declaration of Independence or the cartoons? Why?**

5. Assess Distribute ⊘ **Assessment 1.4,** which asks students to identify influences that led to the Revolutionary War and the establishment of a new government.

EXTEND THE LESSON ▬▬▬▬▬▬▬▬

> **L3 Differentiate** Have partners choose another of the listed grievances from the Declaration of Independence, and sketch a political cartoon that conveys its message.

> **L4 Differentiate** Have students create a political cartoon on their own.

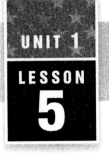

UNIT 1
LESSON
5

The Articles of Confederation

TEACHER INSTRUCTIONS

PURPOSE

To frame an answer to the ✪ **Essential Question:** *What should be the goals of government?*, students should understand the problems that developed under the government formed by the Articles of Confederation.

LESSON GOALS

- Describe the weaknesses of the Articles of Confederation by discussing how they affected the states.
- Discuss the Framers' need to create a new Constitution by discussing the failures of the Articles.

MATERIALS

- ⦿ **Online Student Edition** and copies of ⦿ **Background Notes 1.5A** and **1.5B**, located at PearsonSuccessNet.com
- *Essential Questions Journal*
- Copies of ⦿ **Activity 1.5,** *Government Under the Articles of Confederation,* available at PearsonSuccessNet.com
- Copies of ⦿ **Assessment 1.5,** located at PearsonSuccessNet.com

BEFORE CLASS

Distribute copies of ⦿ **Background Notes 1.5A** and **1.5B.** For more in-depth information, refer students to the ⦿ **Online Student Edition** Chapter 2, Section 3. You may wish to have students read these materials before coming to class. You may also want students to complete the *Essential Questions Journal* Warmup, p. 11, and Chapter 2 Exploration, p. 12, before class.

> **L2 Differentiate** Ask students to write down 3–5 main ideas from each Background Note, exchange them with a partner, and agree on three main points to share with the class. Write these points on the board and help students select those that create the most accurate summary.

> **L2 Differentiate** Have students listen to the online summary, available at PearsonSuccessNet.com.

TEACH

1. Build Background Ask students why the states established as their government a confederation "a firm league of friendship" with a congress (but no executive or judicial branches) after the American Revolution. *(The states feared an executive branch with too much power because of their experiences with Britain's powerful and unresponsive monarchy; the states guarded their rights jealously.)*

2. Introduce the Lesson Pass out the ⊘Background Notes 1.5A and 1.5B. Explain to students that they will be creating a game in order to understand how these weaknesses affected the new states, and why the Framers chose to create the Constitution.

3. Complete the Activity Explain that students will be working together to create a game called "Government Under the Articles of Confederation." Students' games should reflect the weaknesses and challenges presented by the Articles of Confederation. For example, the point of the game might involve trying to pass a bill or act to benefit one or many states. These games might be electronic games, board games, strategy games, card games, a combination of these types, or some other type. The games might include objects such as spinners, timers, play money, tiles, game pieces, etc. Have students work in pairs to make a descriptive outline of their games, using ⊘Activity 1.5. Explain that they should use the Background Notes to help them. Their outlines should include the point of the game, the basic rules, the type of game, and any "extras" needed to play the game.

4. Debrief Have volunteers share their outlines and answer questions about their games. Encourage them to tell what they learned about the Articles of Confederation by creating a game that reflects the weaknesses of that government. Invite discussion about similarities and differences in student games.

5. Assess Distribute ⊘Assessment 1.5, which asks students to identify three weaknesses of the confederation that the Framers probably needed to address at the Philadelphia Convention of 1787, where they framed a new constitution that would become the basis for our current government.

EXTEND THE LESSON

L3 Differentiate Have students create the "Government Under the Articles of Confederation" game that they outlined for the activity in this lesson. Allow time for students to play the different games and comment on what they learned from each one.

L4 Differentiate Have students research Shays's Rebellion. Ask them to write a short essay explaining how this incident reflected the need for a new form of government.

UNIT 1

LESSON 6

TEACHER INSTRUCTIONS

PURPOSE

To frame an answer to the 🍂 Essential Question: *What should be the goals of government?,* students should take on the interests of an 18th-century state, create a constitution, and join with other states to debate and create their own national constitution.

LESSON GOALS

- Identify the issues that confronted the Framers of the Constitution.
- Identify the position of a given state on issues the Framers addressed at the Constitutional Convention of 1787.
- Describe the several plans presented at the Constitutional Convention and the compromises that integrated those plans.
- Propose and debate plans that might have been presented by a given state at the Constitutional Convention.
- Compare the class constitution from their simulation with the United States Constitution.

MATERIALS

- 🕖 **Online Student Edition** and copies of 🕖 **Background Notes 1.6A, 1.6B, 1.6C,** and **1.6D,** located at PearsonSuccessNet.com
- *Essential Questions Journal*
- Copies of 🕖 **Activity 1.6A,** *Ten Questions: State Interests,* located at PearsonSuccessNet.com
- Copies of 🕖 **Activity 1.6B,** *Answering the Questions,* located at PearsonSuccessNet.com
- **Constitution: Role Cards 1–6**
- **Constitution 1.a** and **1.b:** *Colonial Industry* and *Slavery in the United States*
- **Constitution 1.c:** *"Remember the Ladies" letter*
- **Constitution 1.d:** *The Providential Detection*
- **Constitution 1.e:** *Build a Constitution*
- **Constitution 1.f:** *Our Constitution*
- Copies of 🕖 **Assessment 1.6,** located at PearsonSuccessNet.com

DAYS 1–2

BEFORE CLASS

Distribute copies of 🕖 **Background Notes 1.6A** and **1.6B.** For more in-depth information, refer students to the 🕖 **Online Student Edition** Chapter 3, Section 1. You may wish to have students read these materials before coming to class. You may also want students to complete the *Essential Questions Journal* Warmup, p. 19, and Chapter 3 Exploration, p. 20, before class.

L2 Differentiate Ask students to write down 3–5 main ideas from each Background Note, exchange them with a partner, and agree on three main points to share with the class. Write these points on the board and help students select those that create the most accurate summary.

L2 Differentiate Have students listen to the online summary, available at PearsonSuccessNet.com.

TEACH

1. Build Background Ask volunteers to recall the major weaknesses of the Articles of Confederation; list them on the board. Then have students write their names under the three weaknesses that they believe were most difficult for the Framers to address at the Constitutional Convention. Invite students to share their thinking and discuss differences.

2. Introduce the Lesson Assign each student to one of six groups. Explain that each group represents one state: (1) Massachusetts (large, northern state); (2) Pennsylvania (large, mid-Atlantic state); (3) Virginia (large, southern state); (4) New Hampshire (small, northern state); (5) Delaware (small, mid-Atlantic state); (6) Georgia (small, southern state). Give each group their corresponding state card, and have students read over the information for their assigned state.

3. Complete the Activity Give each group a copy of ⊘**Activity 1.6A** *Ten Questions: State Interests.* Hang **Constitution 1.a,** *Colonial Industry,* and **Constitution 1.b,** *Slavery in the United States,* on the board. Explain that students will fill out the worksheet by giving the positions of their state on ten questions addressed at the Constitutional Convention of 1787.

Allow each group sufficient time to study and consider **Constitution 1.c,** *Remember the Ladies;* **Constitution 1.d,** *The Providential Detection;* and the excerpts from the *Federalist* and *Anti-Federalist* papers in the next lesson. They might also review their Background Notes on weaknesses of the Articles of Confederation, the *Landmark English Documents,* and the *Enlightenment Philosophers.* Students should also refer to their online or print Student Edition or to other sources. For example, students can find information at their state's official site, or at www.archives.gov.

Have the groups study each map and pass around primary source materials. They should discuss how these sources relate to their state's responses to the ten questions. Point out that the maps can help students understand their state's positions on slavery, representation, and other issues. Point out the correlation between the main industries of each state and the size of its slave population.

Groups should then create a plan for a new constitution, based on their state's position on the ten questions. Each group should consider the best form of government for the nation, as well as their own state. Have them create mini-posters of their constitutional proposals.

4. Debrief Have a volunteer from each group share their responses to ⊘**Activity 1.6A,** *Ten Questions: State Interests.* Encourage students to discuss the issues that divided large and small states, and northern and southern states. Pass out ⊘**Activity 1.6B,** *Answering the Questions.* Have groups fill in the questions that large, small, northern, and southern states answered differently. Then, have them answer the Reflection Questions.

5. Assess Review each group's mini-poster. Ask how students came to their decisions for each question. Then ask them which questions caused debate within their own state, and which questions were answered easily.

DAYS 3–4

BEFORE CLASS

Distribute copies of ⊘**Background Notes 1.6C** and **1.6D.** For more in-depth information, refer students to the ⊘**Online Student Edition** Chapter 2, Section 4. You may wish to have students read these materials before coming to class. You may also want students to complete the *Essential Questions Journal* Warmup, p. 11, and Chapter 2 Exploration, p. 12, before class.

> **L2 Differentiate** Ask students to read aloud and define the terms in boldface. Then have volunteers explain why these terms are important for understanding the Background Notes.

> **L2 Differentiate** Have students listen to the online summary available at PearsonSuccessNet.com.

TEACH

1. Build Background Remind students that there were several issues that the Framers faced in creating their new government. Each state had a wide range of ideas on each issue. Ask, **How might a large southern state and a small northern state address the counting of slaves as part of the state population? Why?**

2. Introduce the Lesson Call on a volunteer from each state group to summarize their plan for a constitution. Have them post these mini-posters on a bulletin board or wall.

3. Complete the Activity Explain to students that they will begin a two-day simulation of the Constitutional Debates, trying to reach compromises on each of the 10 issues based on their state plans. Display **Constitution 1.e,** *Build a Constitution.* Tell students that all six state groups will work together to fill in the poster by writing their ideas on sticky notes and placing them in the correct boxes.

    Act as the presiding officer of the Convention by keeping the debates focused on the 10 issues and recording students' compromises on the poster. Work down the list of issues with the groups. With each issue, ask: **How can we include this in the Constitution in a way that satisfies as many states as possible?** Students should begin to realize that each of the states had different ideas on how they should be represented in Congress, what powers the executive branch should have, and so on. Guide students in coming up with compromises that satisfy as many states' interests as possible. Refer them to ⊘**Background Notes 1.6C** and **1.6D** on the Virginia and New Jersey plans and the Connecticut Compromise, as well as the excerpt from Abigail Adams.

4. Debrief Display **Constitution 1.f,** *Our Constitution.* Review the results of the simulated debate and compromises, and compare the end results with those of the United States Constitution. Call on a different volunteer to read each section from the poster.

5. Assess Distribute ⊘**Assessment 1.6,** which asks students to identify two ways in which their state in 1787 would have benefited from their class constitution and two ways in which it would not have benefited.

EXTEND THE LESSON ━━━━━━━━━

Ask students to research a position presented in *The Federalist* on one issue, such as the power of the presidency. (They might refer to ⊘**Activity 1.6A** *Ten Questions: State Interests* worksheet to choose an issue.) The *Federalist Papers* can be found at the Library of Congress's Web site, thomas. loc.gov. Encourage them to report their findings to the class.

TEACHER INSTRUCTIONS

PURPOSE

To frame an answer to the 🌐 **Essential Question:** *What should be the goals of government?*, students should understand the debates and compromises that took place during the ratification of the Constitution.

LESSON GOALS

* Describe the process through which the Constitution was ratified.
* Explain the controversy over the ratification of the Constitution.

MATERIALS

* 🕜**Online Student Edition** and copies of 🕜**Background Note 1.7,** located at PearsonSuccessNet.com
* *Essential Questions Journal*
* Copies of 🕜**Activity 1.7,** *Federalist and Anti-Federalist Excerpts,* located at PearsonSuccessNet.com
* Copies of 🕜**Assessment 1.7,** located at PearsonSuccessNet.com
* Roles Cards 1–6
* **Constitution 1.e:** *Build a Constitution*
* **Constitution 1.f:** *Our Constitution*

BEFORE CLASS

Distribute copies of 🕜**Background Note 1.7.** For more in-depth information, refer students to the 🕜**Online Student Edition** Chapter 2, Section 4. You may wish to have students read these materials before coming to class. You may also want students to complete the *Essential Questions Journal* Warmup, p. 11, and Chapter 2 Exploration, p. 12, before class.

> **L2 Differentiate** Instead of students reading the Background Note on their own, have volunteers take turns reading portions aloud in class. After each portion is read, have a volunteer other than the reader summarize the information.

> **L2 Differentiate** Have students listen to the online summary, available at PearsonSuccessNet.com.

TEACH

1. Introduce the Lesson Display **Constitution, 1.e:** *Build a Constitution,* and **Constitution, 1.f:** *Our Constitution,* side by side. Explain to students that they will view the portions of United States Constitution that they compared with their class effort. Have volunteers point out the sections in which the class effort came close to what the Framers created.

2. Complete the Activity Have students go back to their state groups and look at their state role cards. Ask: **Was your delegate for or against the ratification of the Constitution?** Have them research information on their states' role in the ratification of the Constitution online or in other sources. You may want to assign the research for homework. Pass out ⨀ **Activity 1.7.** Explain that the *Federalist Papers* and the Anti-Federalist responses were published in newspapers in New York, one of the key states in the ratification process. Have them work through the questions on their activity sheets in groups. Then have each group present a small speech on their state's role in the ratification process.

> **L2 Differentiate** Choose fewer excerpts for students to read, and review difficult terms before students begin. You may wish to work through the excerpts as a class.

3. Debrief Discuss how the Framers addressed objections that the Anti-Federalists had to the Constitution. Point out that the Bill of Rights was only added to the Constitution after the Anti-Federalists refused to ratify.

4. Assess Distribute ⨀ **Assessment 1.7,** which asks students to identify two provisions in the Constitution to which their state objected and two issues it supported.

EXTEND THE LESSON

> **L3 Differentiate** The Framers devoted an entire article, Article VII, to the ratification process. Have students write a one-page essay on why the Framers put so much emphasis on this process.

> **L2 Differentiate** Have students list three reasons why the Framers devoted Article VII to the ratification process.

TEACHER INSTRUCTIONS

PURPOSE

To frame an answer to the 🌐 **Essential Question:** *What should be the goals of government?,* students should recognize the six principles of government laid out by the Constitution.

LESSON GOALS

- Identify examples of how the six basic principles were integrated into the Constitution.

MATERIALS

- 🖉 **Online Student Edition** and copies of 🖉 **Background Note 1.8,** located at PearsonSuccessNet.com
- *Essential Questions Journal*
- Copies of 🖉 **Activity 1.8,** *Constitution Scavenger Hunt,* located at PearsonSuccessNet.com
- Copies of 🖉 **Assessment 1.8,** located at PearsonSuccessNet.com

BEFORE CLASS

Distribute copies of 🖉 **Background Note 1.8.** For more in-depth information, refer students to the 🖉 **Online Student Edition** Chapter 3, Section 1. You may wish to have students read these materials before coming to class. You may also want students to complete the *Essential Questions Journal* Warmup, p. 19, and Chapter 3 Exploration, p. 20, before class.

> **L2 Differentiate** Ask students to read aloud and define the terms in boldface. Then have volunteers explain why these terms are important for understanding the Background Note.

> **L2 Differentiate** Have students listen to the online summary, available at PearsonSuccessNet.com.

TEACH

1. Introduce the Lesson List the six basic principles on the board. Explain to students that the Framers relied on these principles to create a balanced and democratic government.

2. Complete the Activity Refer students to the Constitution in the 🖉 **Online Student Edition,** and have them read 🖉 **Background Note 1.8.** Point out examples of the six principles embedded in the Constitution. Pass out 🖉 **Activity 1.8,** *Constitution Scavenger Hunt,* and have students locate other examples of the six principles. Explain that judicial review is not directly addressed in the Constitution. It was later established by *Marbury* v. *Madison.* Review this case with students.

3. Debrief Refer students to the class constitution. Ask them to find provisions in which the principles appear. Ask students to find ways in which the Framers could have included judicial review.

4. Assess Distribute 🖉 **Assessment 1.8,** which asks students to define each principle and explain how it is applied in the United States system of government.

TEACHER INSTRUCTIONS

PURPOSE

To frame an answer to the 🌐 **Essential Question:** *What should be the goals of government?*, students should understand how the United States government protects citizens' rights and freedom.

LESSON GOALS

- Describe how the Bill of Rights guarantees fundamental civil liberties of all United States citizens.
- Find the locations of specific amendments.
- Explain the amendment process.

MATERIALS

- 🕐**Online Student Edition** and copies of 🕐**Background Notes 1.9A, 1.9B,** and **1.9C,** located at PearsonSuccessNet.com
- *American Government Essential Questions* DVD or 🕐online at PearsonSuccessNet.com.
- *Essential Questions Journal*
- Copies of 🕐*Activity 1.9, Twenty Questions,* located at PearsonSuccessNet.com
- Copies of 🕐**Assessment 1.9,** located at PearsonSuccessNet.com

BEFORE CLASS

Distribute copies of 🕐**Background Notes 1.9A, 1.9B,** and **1.9C.** For more in-depth information, refer students to the 🕐**Online Student Edition** Chapter 3, Sections 2 and 3, and Chapter 4, Sections 1 and 2. You may wish to have students read these materials before coming to class. You may also want students to complete the *Essential Questions Journal* Warmups, pp. 19 and 25, and Chapters 3 and 4 Explorations, pp. 20 and 26, before class.

> **L2 Differentiate** Help students create an outline of the Background Notes by identifying the main idea and supporting details. Write the outlines on the board.

> **L2 Differentiate** Have students listen to the online summary, available at PearsonSuccessNet.com.

TEACH

1. Build Background Point out that the Constitution was written with the expectation of amendment. Display or read aloud Article V of the Constitution. Ask students why the Framers may have created a provision for amending the Constitution. Invite them to think of events in history when the Constitution needed to be amended. Ask them to cite specific amendments they may know.

L2 Differentiate Discuss the definition of the word *amend*, and connect it to the noun *amendment*.

2. Introduce the Lesson Point out that many Framers believed that the Constitution should contain a written guarantee of their fundamental rights. Encourage discussion about why this issue was debated so vehemently. Point out that the Bill of Rights, the first ten amendments to the Constitution, is the result of this debate.

3. Complete the Activity Explain that students will be working with partners to answer 20 questions about the amendments to the United States Constitution. Distribute ⦿**Activity 1.9,** *Twenty Questions,* and allow students 20 minutes to complete the activity. You may wish to show the "Exploring the 27 Amendments" video before students begin this activity.

4. Debrief Have students take turns answering the 20 questions and reading the amendment that answers each one. Point out the years in which the amendments were passed. Discuss with students the events that led up to the amendments being passed. For example, discuss the women's suffrage movements of the late 19th century and early 20th century. You could also point out President Franklin Roosevelt's four terms as president when discussing the 22nd amendment. Ask students how the changing times affect the Constitution. Then ask: **Do you think that the Framers anticipated amendments to the Constitution? How do you know?** *(By creating a simple framework for a Constitution, and writing in a process of amendment, the Framers anticipated amendments to the Constitution as the country changed.)*

5. Assess Distribute ⦿**Assessment 1.9,** which asks students to name the three constitutional amendments which affect them most and to explain why.

EXTEND THE LESSON

    L2 Differentiate Work with students to understand the rights and protections listed in the Bill of Rights. If students have recently arrived in the U.S., they may not be familiar with some of the rights that Americans hold under the Bill of Rights.

    L3 Differentiate Have students create a chart comparing the Bill of Rights with the English Bill of Rights.

    L4 Differentiate Using the Library of Congress Web site, the National Archives Web site, or other sources, have students choose one of the rights or protections listed in the Bill of Rights and research its origin. Where did this right or protection first appear? Who wrote about it? How did it become part of the Bill of Rights. Have students share their findings with the class.

UNIT 1

LESSON 10

Wrap-Up

TEACHER INSTRUCTIONS

PURPOSE

To frame an answer to the ✦ **Essential Question:** *What should be the goals of government?*, students should reflect on and respond to the Framers' ideas about the following goals.

LESSON GOALS

- Identify and rank the fundamental goals of government and explain their criteria.
- Identify the goals of the United States government as asserted in the Preamble to the Constitution.

MATERIALS

- **⊘ Online Student Edition,** located at PearsonSuccessNet.com
- **Essential Questions Journal**
- Copies of **⊘ Assessment 1.10,** located at PearsonSuccessNet.com

BEFORE CLASS

Refer students to the **⊘ Online Student Edition** Chapter 1, Section 1, and Chapter 4, Sections 2 and 3. You may wish to have students read these materials before coming to class. You may also want students to complete the **Essential Questions Journal** Warmups, pp. 2 and 25, and Chapters 1 and 4 Explorations, pp. 3 and 26, before class.

> **L2 Differentiate** Have students listen to the online summary, available at PearsonSuccessNet.com.

TEACH

1. Introduce the Lesson Write the Preamble to the Constitution on the board. Call on a volunteer to read it. Then ask students to identify the purpose of the Preamble. *(to introduce the Constitution by setting forth the goals of the United States government)*

2. Complete the Activity Explain that partners will be working together over the next 20 minutes to list the six goals of the United States government as set out in the Preamble. They will also rank these goals in order of importance and give a rationale for their ranking.

3. Debrief Have a volunteer from each pair identify one of the goals of government they identified. List the six goals on the board. Then have pairs give their ranking of these goals. Keep a tally of these rankings by allotting 1 to 6 marks to a goal, based on each student response. Encourage discussion about the results of this survey.

4. Assess Distribute **⊘ Assessment 1.10,** which asks students to use their learning from this lesson to answer questions about the goals of government.

Have students answer the ✿ **Essential Question:** *What should be the goals of government?*, in their *Essential Questions Journal.* You may also use one of the following formats:

- Write an essay.
- Present the answer in a multimedia format.
- Present the answer in a visual format.
- Create a skit that shows the various goals that government should achieve.

EXTEND THE LESSON ▬▬▬▬▬▬▬▬▬▬

L3 Differentiate Ask students to create a skit that involves one or more students meeting with a time-traveling Thomas Jefferson. They should keep in mind Jefferson's inaugural remark: "A wise and frugal government shall restrain men from injuring one another, shall leave them otherwise free to regulate their own pursuits of industry and improvement, and shall not take from the mouth of labor the bread it has earned. This is the sum of good government." Student skits could address the following questions: Did Jefferson expect the Constitution to be so successful? Why or why not? How does he explain its success? Is he pleased or disappointed by amendments that were added later? Why or why not? How does he feel about the size and power of today's United States government?

UNIT 2

Political Behavior: Government By the People

UNIT OVERVIEW

This group of lessons teaches your students about the role of elections in the American system of government and about the many opportunities elections provide citizens for participation in the political and civic life of the nation. The lessons culminate in a classroom mock political campaign. At the end of this unit, students will be able to craft an answer to the ✪ **Essential Question**, *In what ways should people participate in public affairs?* You may wish to have students begin their study by completing the *Essential Questions Journal* Unit 2 Warmup, p. 35.

UNIT GOALS

- Analyze the value of political and civic participation in the United States.
- Understand the various avenues for political participation.
- Understand the electoral process.
- Use media literacy and analysis skills to consider the role of public opinion and the media in our democracy.
- Develop a well-informed and well-executed campaign strategy for a candidate for office.

TIME ALLOTMENT

This unit of activities is intended to be taught in 12 days (or 6 days on a block schedule).

DAY 1	Lesson 1	Informed Citizenship
DAY 2	Lesson 2	Voting
DAY 3	Lesson 3	Knowing the Voters
DAY 4	Lesson 4	Deciding on the Candidates
DAY 5	Lesson 5	Interactive Decision-Making: Understanding the Electoral College
DAY 6	Lesson 6	The Media in Politics
DAY 7	Lesson 7	Speaking to the Media
DAY 8	Lesson 8	Advertising and the Media
DAY 9	Lesson 9	Money and Politics
DAY 10–12	Lesson 10	Political Campaign

ENDURING UNDERSTANDINGS

- Our political system depends on the active involvement of informed citizens who take part in elections and help shape public policy.
- Voting is an important way for informed citizens to be involved in public life.
- The media has a significant impact on the way voters think and behave.
- By understanding the way media impacts people, citizens can become better informed.
- Money is a powerful and potentially problematic influence in our political system.

UNIT 2

LESSON 1

TEACHER INSTRUCTIONS

PURPOSE

To frame an answer to the 🌐 **Essential Question,** *In what ways should people participate in public affairs?* students need to know what role citizens play in a democratic system, and what they need to do to effectively fill that role.

LESSON GOALS

- Demonstrate understanding of the roles and responsibilities of citizens in a democratic system by analyzing a video and by finding examples in the media.
- Analyze citizens' roles and responsibilities through classroom discussion.

MATERIALS

- 🖉 **Online Student Edition** and copies of 🖉 **Background Notes 2.1A, 2.1B** and **2.1C,** located at PearsonSuccessNet.com
- *Essential Questions Journal*
- *American Government Essential Questions Video* DVD or online at PearsonSuccessNet.com
- Newspapers, magazines, history books, or other print or online reference material with historic or current national and international news and images
- Copies of 🖉 **Activity 2.1,** *Roles and Responsibilities of Citizenship,* located at PearsonSuccessNet.com
- Copies of 🖉 **Assessment 2.1,** located at PearsonSuccessNet.com

BEFORE CLASS

Distribute copies of 🖉 **Background Notes 2.1A** and **2.1B.** For more in-depth information, refer students to the 🖉 **Online Student Edition** Chapter 8, Section 1. You may wish to have students read these materials before coming to class. You may also want students to complete the *Essential Questions Journal* Chapter 8 Warmup, p. 59, and Chapter 8 Exploration I, p. 60, before class.

L2 Differentiate Have students listen to the online summary located at PearsonSuccessNet.com

L4 Differentiate Distribute 🖉 **Background Note 2.1C,** which provides a historical overview of civics and political participation in the United States. Ask students to summarize the main points of the note for the class. Discuss reasons why the 2008 presidential election sparked an increase in political participation. Ask: **What circumstances would encourage this trend to continue?**

TEACH

1. Activate Prior Knowledge Tell students that the goal of this unit is to explore the
🌐 Essential Question: *In what ways should people participate in public affairs?* To help them
start thinking about this question, have them to review their answers to the *Essential Questions
Journal* Unit 2 Warmup, p. 35, in which they explored the responsibilities of citizenship. If they
have not already completed the Warmup activity, have them complete the assignment in class.

2. Introduce the Lesson Show students the Unit 2 segment of the *American Government
Essential Questions Video,* which focuses on voting and other ways that Americans can
participate in government. Make a list on the board of the kinds of civic participation with which
students are familiar. Ask them how they can participate now and how they see themselves
participating in the future.

Review 🖉Background Note 2.1A. Explain that a democratic system places significant
responsibilities on its citizens. Ask students what would happen if the citizens in a democracy were
unable or unwilling to fulfill their responsibilities. You may also wish to ask what would happen if
only those who are well-informed were allowed to participate, and discuss the arguments for and
against that idea. Would such a requirement encourage people to become better informed?

3. Complete the Activity Review 🖉Background Note 2.B. Then have students look for
examples in newspapers and magazines of ways in which citizens meet and fulfill the various roles
and responsibilities that are at the heart of citizenship. You may wish to assign this research for
homework prior to beginning the lesson. Alternatively, you may wish to provide students with
specific examples. Rather than using print materials, you may refer students to online news
sources or to the many Web sites that focus on citizen participation. Distribute 🖉Activity 2.1 and
have students work in pairs to follow the directions on the worksheet. Describe the examples they
found, identify the roles to which each example applies, and indicate any secondary role that may
also apply. Circulate among students to answer questions and keep them focused.

> **L2 Differentiate** Review the different roles and responsibilities of citizenship. Before
> students begin scanning the available materials, provide some examples to help them better
> understand the concepts. Then brainstorm some examples they might look for as they page
> through the assembled materials. For example, for "Tolerating Differences," they might look
> for pictures of people of different skin colors or age groups or languages working together.
> For "Expressing an Opinion Publicly," they might show a letter to an editor or an image of a
> street protest.

4. Debrief Invite students to share their answers to the first two Reflection Questions at the end
of **Activity 2.1** worksheet as a class. Keep a tally on the board of which roles or responsibilities are
mentioned. Then discuss the results. Was there general agreement among the class about which
roles and responsibilities were most important and which were most difficult to fill? Were there
wide differences? Help students recognize that all the roles and responsibilities are essential to the
long-term health and functioning of our society.

5. Assess Distribute 🖉Assessment 2.1, in which students write captions for each of the
photographs or images they found that illustrate the roles and responsibilities of citizenship.

EXTEND THE LESSON ▬▬▬▬▬▬▬▬▬▬

> **L3 Differentiate** Have students write a one-paragraph introduction for a new-citizen
> brochure that explains the need for citizens in the United States to be informed and to
> know their rights and responsibilities.

TEACHER INSTRUCTIONS

PURPOSE

To frame an answer to the 🌐 **Essential Question,** *In what ways should people participate in public affairs?,* students need to know the central role of voting in a democratic society and what they need to do to fulfill this responsibility.

LESSON GOALS

- Discuss the importance of voting, and explore the history of voting rights in the United States through explaining events on a timeline.
- Examine voting procedures and requirements by playing a voting game with a partner.

MATERIALS

- 🕙 **Online Student Edition** and copies of 🕙 **Background Notes 2.2A** and **2.2B,** located at PearsonSuccessNet.com
- ***Essential Questions Journal***
- Copies of 🕙 **Activity 2.2,** *Voting Game,* located at PearsonSuccessNet.com
- Copies of 🕙 **Assessment 2.2,** located at PearsonSuccessNet.com

BEFORE CLASS

Distribute copies of 🕙 **Background Notes 2.2A** and **2.2B.** For more in-depth information, refer students to the 🕙 **Online Student Edition** Chapter 5, Section 1; Chapter 6, Section 1; and Chapter 7, Section 2. You may wish to have students read these materials before coming to class. You may also want students to complete the ***Essential Questions Journal*** Chapter 5 Explorations I and II, pp. 37–38, and Chapter 6 Warmup, Explorations, and Essay, pp. 43–50, before class.

> **L2 Differentiate** Instead of students reading the Background Notes on their own, have volunteers take turns reading portions aloud in class. After each portion is read, have a volunteer other than the reader summarize the information.

> **L2 Differentiate** Have students listen to the online summary located at PearsonSuccessNet.com

TEACH

1. Activate Prior Knowledge Remind students that the goal of this unit is to explore the **Essential Question,** *In What Ways Should People Participate in Public Affairs?* Ask them to recall what they learned in Lesson 1 about the different ways people take part in public life. Remind them that voting is one of the key responsibilities of citizens. Ask: **Why is voting so important to our democratic society?** *(The will of the people is communicated to elected leaders. Active, knowledgeable voters help make government of, by, and for the people possible.)*

2. Introduce the Lesson Tell students that since the country's founding, there has been a steady expansion of voting rights, with suffrage expanding to include a larger and larger share of the electorate. At this time, ask students to review ◯ **Background Note 2.2A,** which gives some of the highlights of this historical trend. Explain that the exercise of suffrage is limited to those who meet certain specific requirements, including those for citizenship, age, and residency. To help reinforce this concept, you may review ◯ **Background Note 2.2B.** Point out that those wishing to vote must generally go through a process of registration, which varies from state to state but follows the same basic process. Finally, the successful exercise of suffrage requires some knowledge of the voting process—where, how, and when to cast a ballot. Ask students what kinds of skill and knowledge might be necessary to be a voter today. Then ask whether they think the demands placed on voters discourage their participation.

3. Complete the Activity Distribute ◯ **Activity 2.2,** *Voting Game.* Tell students that they will now spend 20 minutes playing a game that tests their knowledge about voting procedures and requirements. Students will play in teams, taking turns answering questions and confirming answers. Encourage the answer-checkers to be thorough and precise in checking the answers of their game partners. Circulate among students to ensure they stay focused, to answer questions, and to settle disputes about answers.

> **L2 Differentiate** Review definitions before students begin to play. You may also wish to pair L2 students with L3 and L4 students for this activity.

4. Debrief Invite students to share the results of their game: How did they rate their knowledge of the terms and concepts of voting? Did they get most of the questions right on the first attempt? Were the answers thorough and complete?

5. Assess Distribute copies of ◯ **Assessment 2.2.** For the assessment, arrange students in groups of 3–5. Have them follow instructions for engaging in a discussion and completing the memo-writing activity. You may wish to assign the memo-writing activity for homework.

EXTEND THE LESSON ▬▬▬▬

> **L3 Differentiate** Have students research the specific voting registration and voting requirements in their community. Based on their findings, ask them to produce a set of step-by-step instructions that detail: • When to register • How to register • Where to register • Where to vote • When to vote

> **L4 Differentiate** Have students find out what types of voting machines or methods are used in their community and provide information about how these machines work. Students can obtain information from local government offices or the Internet.

UNIT 2

LESSON 3

Knowing the Voters

TEACHER INSTRUCTIONS

PURPOSE

The 🌐 **Essential Question,** *In what ways should people participate in public affairs?* requires an understanding of the many levels on which modern political campaigns function and the many levels on which they seek to understand and reach voters.

LESSON GOALS

- Explore the many factors that might influence a person's voting decisions through discussion and by analyzing recent election results.
- Analyze information about the students' state and the preferences of its voters by collecting state data and writing a state profile.
- Analyze how the students' state features might influence and shape a political campaign to reach the state's voters by writing a memo to a candidate.

MATERIALS

- 🖉 **Online Student Edition** and copies of 🖉 **Background Notes 2.3A** and **2.3B,** located at PearsonSuccessNet.com
- *Essential Questions Journal*
- Copies of 🖉 **Activity 2.3,** *Knowing the Voters,* located at PearsonSuccessNet.com
- Internet access and written materials about your state, such as atlases and census reports
- Copies of 🖉 **Assessment 2.3** located at PearsonSuccessNet.com

BEFORE CLASS

Distribute copies of 🖉 **Background Notes 2.3A** and **2.3B.** For more in-depth information, refer students to the 🖉 **Online Student Edition,** Chapter 6, Section 4. You may wish to have students read these materials before coming to class. You may also want students to review their responses to the *Essential Questions Journal* Chapter 6 Exploration IV.

> **L2 Differentiate** Ask volunteers to explain the main idea of each Background Note. Write this information on the board for students to keep in mind as they complete the lesson.

> **L2 Differentiate** Have students listen to the online summary located at PearsonSuccessNet.com

TEACH

1. Build Background Remind students that a key avenue for civic participation in the United States is elections—both voting and taking part in the effort to elect a candidate. Explain that at its core, the effort to elect a candidate is really an effort to connect with the voters about issues that matter to them. Ask: **How can candidates and political campaigns learn about the needs and**

wants of voters? *(They can learn about the state or district, they can talk to the voters, they can take polls.)*

2. Introduce the Lesson Explain that candidates and political campaigns must seek to understand the voters they hope to win. As part of this process, they must learn about the broad characteristics of the place they want to represent. This involves learning about people and culture, and about the unique issues and challenges they face. With that information, candidates and their campaigns can craft an approach that is most likely to win support. Refer students to ✆Background Notes 2.3A and 2.3B. Ask: **Which do you believe is more important to voters, their party affiliation or individual candidates and issues? Which should be more important? Why?** You may wish to follow up by leading a discussion about the influence of party affiliation. Then direct students' attention to the chart "Voting By Groups in the 2008 Presidential Election" and ask volunteers to summarize the information. *(Women voted Democratic slightly more than did men; more whites voted Republican than Democratic, but minorities voted Democratic by overwhelming majorities; younger voters voted Democratic by wide margins, while voters 65 and older tended to vote Republican.)* Discuss reasons for these voting patterns. Then ask: **How might a future candidate use this information?** *(by targeting the specific concerns of the various groups)*

3. Complete the Activity Distribute ✆Activity 2.3. Explain that students will now spend some time researching their own state and the needs and wishes of its voters so that they can gather information for a state-wide political campaign. You may wish to assign this research as homework or allow students a second class period to complete this activity. Have students work individually to review sources and collect information, as directed in the activity.

> **L3 Differentiate** If you would like a shorter activity, suggest that students use the following issues instead of researching specific issues for their state: **(1)** shortfalls in the state budget, **(2)** underperforming schools in urban areas, **(3)** the increasing burdens on many state residents of rising fuel and gasoline costs. Alternatively, you may wish to brainstorm state issues as a class.

> **L2 Differentiate** Allow students to work in small groups to search for and collect information and write their profiles.

> **L4 Differentiate** Have students research their county or equivalent rather than their state.

4. Debrief Discuss students' findings about their state or county. Invite students to read their profiles, and discuss student reactions to each other's characterization. Ask: **How does the profile of the state affect a political campaign?** *(It would help determine what issues the campaign would stress, and it might affect how the campaign seeks to reach voters.)*

NOTE: Be sure to save the state profiles. Students may use them in a future activity.

5. Assess Distribute ✆Assessment 2.3. Arrange students in groups of 3 to 5 to complete the discussion and memo-writing activity.

EXTEND THE LESSON ━━━━━━━━━

> **L3 Differentiate** Have students conduct additional research about the particular demographic and economic features of their congressional district and write a summary of their findings that compares and contrasts their district to the rest of the state.

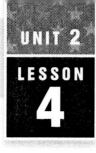

TEACHER INSTRUCTIONS

PURPOSE

To frame an answer to the ✦ **Essential Question,** *In what ways should people participate in public affairs?,* students need to know that before voters can make their voices heard in a general election, candidates must be identified and selected. An understanding of how we nominate candidates is essential knowledge for active citizens.

LESSON GOAL

- Explore the purpose and importance of nomination through teacher-led discussion and an in-class primary campaign and election.

MATERIALS

- ⊘**Online Student Edition** and copies of ⊘**Background Notes 2.4A** and **2.4B,** located at PearsonSuccessNet.com
- *Essential Questions Journal*
- Copies of ⊘**Activity 2.4,** *In-Class Primary,* located at PearsonSuccessNet.com
- Strips of paper (enough for a ballot for each member of the class)
- Copies of ⊘**Assessment 2.4,** located at PearsonSuccessNet.com

BEFORE CLASS

Distribute copies of ⊘**Background Notes 2.4A** and **2.4B.** For more in-depth information, refer students to the ⊘**Online Student Edition,** Chapter 7, Section 1. You may wish to have students read these materials before coming to class. You may also want students to complete the *Essential Questions Journal* Chapter 7 Exploration I, pp. 52–53 before class.

> **L2 Differentiate** Ask volunteers to read aloud and explain the bold-faced terms in the Background Notes. Explain any additional words in the Notes that students identify as unfamiliar.

> **L2 Differentiate** Have students listen to the online summary located at PearsonSuccessNet.com

TEACH

1. Activate Prior Knowledge Remind students that the goal of this unit is to explore the ✦ **Essential Question,** *In what ways should people participate in public affairs?* Ask them to recall what they have learned about the importance of voting and taking part in elections. Ask: **What would happen if the quality of candidates available to voters in an election were poor?** *(Voters would elect a poor candidate for office. The quality of government might suffer.)* **What does that fact suggest about the importance of choosing good candidates?** *(Choosing good candidates is essential to the quality of government.)*

2. Introduce the Lesson Explain that representative democracy is only as strong as the candidates who seek and win election to government posts. For this reason, the process of nominating candidates to run for election is a key step in the democratic process. In this country, we use a variety of methods to choose our candidates. For many major offices, the most widely used process is the direct primary. This is an election in which voters choose from among two or more candidates who are seeking to win a place on the ballot in the general election.

3. Complete the Activity Explain that students will now spend some time conducting a mock primary election in the classroom. Divide the class into teams of 3–4 students. Distribute **Activity 2.4,** *In-Class Primary.* After students have had an opportunity to develop their profiles, direct the class to listen to each team's presentation. Be sure each team listens to and records information about the other teams' candidates. Tell students to note especially each candidate's party. Explain that the primary is a contest within the party—that is, Democrats are running against Democrats, and Republicans are running against Republicans.

Next, have the teams write their campaign speeches. Remind students to keep their speeches brief. Then direct the class to listen to each team's speeches.

Finally, give students a chance to vote on the candidates. Instruct the class that individuals are not allowed to vote for their own candidates. They can, however, vote for a candidate of any party. Have students record their votes on small strips of paper. Collect the strips, count the votes, and announce the top vote getters in each party.

4. Debrief Discuss the results of the primary election with the class. Ask each team to explain how they sought to attract voters. Ask voters to explain what influenced their votes. Explain that in a primary election, voters may be deciding among candidates who share similar ideas and backgrounds. What other factors might influence voters in such a case?

NOTE: Be sure to keep the profiles of the top candidates. Students will use these profiles in future activities.

5. Assess Distribute **Assessment 2.4,** which asks students to answer a series of Reflection Questions that explore the process of nomination and primary elections.

EXTEND THE LESSON

L3 Differentiate Have students write a position paper for their candidate on an issue of concern for people in your state. It could be a national issue, such as taxes or climate change, or something of more regional or state-specific concern. Remind students that their position paper should be designed to appeal to people of their own candidate's party.

L4 Differentiate Political parties play a major role in all but a few local elections. Yet the Framers were worried about the development of political parties, or "factions." Ask students to use their textbooks and other sources to research to help them frame answers to the following questions. You may wish to have them report the results of their research and thinking to the class: What worried the Framers about "factions"? Were their worries justified? Was the development of political parties inevitable? How do political parties aid the democratic process? How might they hinder it?

UNIT 2
LESSON
5

**Interactive Decision-Making:
Understanding the Electoral College**

TEACHER INSTRUCTIONS

PURPOSE

To help gain an understanding of the electoral college, students will take on the role of a campaign strategist determining how his or her candidate should proceed in order to win the presidency.

LESSON GOAL

- Explain how the electoral college determines the outcome of a presidential race.
- Understand the strategy and tactics of presidential campaign strategists through exploring various electoral college scenarios.

MATERIALS

- **Online Interactive Decision-Making,** located at PearsonSuccessNet.com
- *Essential Questions Journal*

BEFORE CLASS

Refer students to the **Online Student Edition** Chapter 13, Sections 5. You may wish to have students read this material before coming to class. You may also want students to complete the *Essential Questions Journal* Chapter 13 Exploration III, p. 107, before class.

TEACH

1. Introduce the Lesson Make sure that students understand that Americans do not vote directly for President, but cast their votes for presidential electors. Each state has as many electors as it has members of Congress. The winning candidate customarily receives all of the state's electoral votes. Write the following question on the board: **Can a candidate become President without winning the largest number of popular votes?** Explain that several Presidents have won the popular vote, but lost in the electoral college and thus failed to become President.

2. Complete the Activity Have students complete the online activity in class or assign it as homework. NOTE: If you decide to give this as a homework assignment, conduct the Debrief at the beginning of class and then continue with the next day's lesson plan.

3. Debrief Once students have completed the online interactivity, ask them to compare their experiences. What strategies were most successful? Why? Point out that many people have called for abolishing the electoral college in favor of direct popular election. Discuss whether, based on their reading and the interactivity, direct popular election would be a better choice for electing the President.

4. Assess Have students write 3–5 conclusions they can draw about the electoral college from the online activity. You may wish to have students share these conclusions in class.

UNIT 2

LESSON

6

The Media in Politics

TEACHER INSTRUCTIONS

PURPOSE

To frame an answer to the 🌐 **Essential Question,** *In what ways should people participate in public affairs?* students need to know the powerful influence of the media in American political life and the ways in which media coverage can impact a political campaign.

LESSON GOALS

- Explain the role of "earned" media in a political campaign.
- Write a press release to demonstrate understanding of the importance of media coverage to political campaigns.

MATERIALS

- 🖉 **Online Student Edition** and copies of 🖉 **Background Notes 2.6A, 2.6B,** and **2.6C,** located at PearsonSuccessNet.com
- *Essential Questions Journal*
- Copies of 🖉 **Activity 2.6 Part I,** *Sample Press Release* and **2.6 Part II,** *Writing a Press Release,* located at PearsonSuccessNet.com
- Copies of 🖉 **Assessment 2.6,** located at PearsonSuccessNet.com

BEFORE CLASS

Distribute copies of 🖉 **Background Notes 2.6A, 2.6B,** and **2.6C.** For more in-depth information, refer students to the 🖉 **Online Student Edition** Chapter 8, Section 3. You may wish to have students read these materials before coming to class. You may also want students to complete the *Essential Questions Journal* Chapter 8 Exploration III, What Have You Learned, and Chapter Essay, pp. 62–65, before class.

> **L2 Differentiate** Before students read the Background Notes, explain any complex vocabulary or concepts.

> **L2 Differentiate** Have students listen to the audio summary available at PearsonSuccessNet.com

TEACH

1. Build Background Tell students that the mass media—those means of communication that reach large, widely dispersed audiences—are the primary means by which the public receives information about public affairs and makes decisions such as how to vote. If they have not already, have students read 🖉 **Background Note 2.6A** to learn about the role of media in politics. Then use 🖉 **Background Note 2.6B** to discuss the difference between earned media and paid media. Ask: **What is the difference between earned and paid media?** *(Earned media is that which is not* *paid for—for example, news coverage of a campaign event. Paid media includes campaign commercials or other forms of media for which a person or group pays.)*

2. Introduce the Lesson Distribute ✦**Activity 2.6, Part I,** *Sample Press Release.* Tell students that a press release is a way for an individual or group to inform the press about a newsworthy event. A well-written and well-constructed press release can attract media attention and lead to earned media coverage. Learning to write a good press release is an important skill for citizens who wish to take an active role in public affairs—whether it be in a political campaign or an interest group. In addition, learning how campaigns use press releases makes citizens more media-literate and capable of approaching media in a critical way. Discuss the purpose of the sample press release and its characteristics, including its brevity.

3. Complete the Activity Next, distribute ✦**Activity 2.6, Part II,** *Writing a Press Release.* Have students use the worksheet to write their own press release about a hypothetical campaign event.

L2 Differentiate Allow students to work in pairs to construct their press release.

4. Debrief Have students share their press releases with the rest of the class. After each student has read his or her press release, invite students to offer their opinions as to the effectiveness of the press release. What are its main strengths? What are some suggestions for improvement? Remind students to use the criteria for a press release presented in the activity.

5. Assess Distribute ✦**Assessment 2.6,** which has students answer a series of reflection questions that explore the importance of earned media.

EXTEND THE LESSON ▬▬▬▬▬▬▬

L3 Differentiate Have students review ✦**Background Note 2.6C.** Ask them to use the information about bias in the news media and the Bias Test at the end of the note to evaluate at least 3 news sources (newspapers, news magazines, TV news, or Internet news sources) for one week and report to the class on the differences among the three sources and whether or not any revealed bias.

L2 Differentiate Have students find an example of a press release to bring to class. Ask them to summarize the purpose of the press release and evaluate its effectiveness on a scale of 1–10.

L4 Differentiate Ask students to watch a current political skit or a skit from the recent presidential campaign. Then have them write and perform a political skit for the class.

UNIT 2

LESSON 7

Speaking to the Media

TEACHER INSTRUCTIONS

PURPOSE

To help students frame an answer to the 🏛 **Essential Question,** *In what ways should people participate in public affairs?,* this lesson will continue the exploration of the media and how interaction with it can impact a political campaign.

LESSON GOALS

- Examine the special challenges of communication through television and related media by preparing for a mock television news program.
- Practice communicating effectively in a simulated television talk show.

MATERIALS

- 🖳 **Online Student Edition** and copies of 📄 **Background Notes 2.7A** and **2.7B**, located at PearsonSuccessNet.com
- *Essential Questions Journal*
- Copies of 📄 **Activity 2.7,** *Mock Television News Question-and-Answer Program,* located at PearsonSuccessNet.com
- State profiles from Day 3, Lesson 3, **Activity 2.3**
- Candidate profiles from Day 4, Lesson 4, **Activity 2.4**
- Copies of 📄 **Assessment 2.7,** located at PearsonSuccessNet.com

BEFORE CLASS

Distribute copies of 📄 **Background Note 2.7A** and **Background Note 2.7B.** For more in-depth information, refer students to the 🖳 **Online Student Edition** Chapter 8, Section 3. You may wish to have students read these materials before coming to class. You may also want students to review their responses to the *Essential Questions Journal* Chapter 8, Exploration III, pp. 62–63.

> **L2 Differentiate** Read one or both of the Background Notes aloud to the class. Stop to review any complex vocabulary or concepts.

> **L2 Differentiate** Have students listen to the audio summary available at PearsonSuccessNet.com

TEACH

1. Activate Prior Knowledge Remind students of what they learned in the previous lesson: The mass media—those means of communication that reach large, widely dispersed audiences—are the primary means by which the public receives information about public affairs and makes decisions such as how to vote. Ask: **From what sources do you get the information you receive about public affairs?** List responses on the board. Then lead a discussion about why students rely on these particular forms of media, what types of information they receive, and whether they detect any bias in the media that they use regularly.

2. Introduce the Lesson Tell students that for millions of Americans, television and the Internet are the main sources of news and information about public issues. Review ⍉**Background Note 2.7A,** which provides information about television news media. Next tell students that politicians and political campaigns recognize the power of television, and they work hard to master its potential—and to avoid its pitfalls. Review ⍉**Background Note 2.7B,** which discusses the power of the Internet to spread news to millions of people immediately.

3. Complete the Activity Next distribute ⍉**Activity 2.7,** *Mock Television News Question-and-Answer Program,* in which students stage a brief mock question-and-answer session in order to explore how skillful use of television can help a candidate—and how improper use can hurt. For the activity, divide the class into teams of 4–6 students. Give teams time to assign roles and prepare for the presentation. Provide each team with a copy of the candidate profiles that they produced on Day 4, Lesson 4, **Activity 2.4.** Also distribute to teams their state profiles, which they produced on Day 3, Lesson 3, **Activity 2.3.** Students will use these resources to help frame answers to their questions. After students have had some time to prepare, have each team present its own five-minute question-and-answer session. The rest of the class will serve as the audience for the presentations.

4. Debrief After each presentation, invite the audience to comment on the performance. Ask: **Did you understand the candidate's answers? Did any candidate sound especially persuasive? Did any candidate make a gaffe or other mistake that might trouble voters? Were there some good "sound bites" that might help a candidate gain favorable attention on the news?**

5. Assess Distribute ⍉**Assessment 2.7** and arrange students into small groups in order to discuss responses to discussion questions and then write a brief essay.

EXTEND THE LESSON

L3 Differentiate Have students write a two-paragraph news summary of the question-and-answer session, including quotations from the candidates.

UNIT 2

LESSON 8

Advertising and the Media

TEACHER INSTRUCTIONS

PURPOSE

To frame an answer to the ✪ **Essential Question**, *In what ways should people participate in public affairs?*, students need to know that political campaigns are sometimes at the mercy of media coverage. Campaigns also have the capability of using the media to their own advantage through the use of advertising.

LESSON GOALS

- Explain the role of "paid" media in a political campaign.
- Demonstrate understanding of the role of advertising in political campaigns by writing a campaign commercial script.

MATERIALS

- ⊘**Online Student Edition** and copies of ⊘**Background Note 2.8,** located at PearsonSuccessNet.com
- Computer access
- *Essential Questions Journal*
- Copies of ⊘**Activity 2.8,** *Television Commercial Script,* located at PearsonSuccessNet.com
- State profiles from Day 3, Lesson 3, **Activity 2.3**
- Candidate profiles from Day 4, Lesson 4, **Activity 2.4**
- Copies of ⊘**Assessment 2.8,** located at PearsonSuccessNet.com

BEFORE CLASS

Distribute copies of ⊘**Background Note 2.8.** For more in-depth information, refer students to the ⊘**Online Student Edition** Chapter 8, Section 3. You may wish to have students read these materials before coming to class. You may also want students to review their earlier responses to the *Essential Questions Journal* Chapter 8 Exploration III, pp. 62–63.

> **L2 Differentiate** Explain the three major types of campaign ads before students read the Background Note and ask them to describe actual and fictional examples.

> **L2 Differentiate** Have students listen to the audio summary available at PearsonSuccessNet.com

TEACH

1. Build Background Review with students what they have learned about earned media. Explain that candidates and political campaigns can also pay for media time. Review ⊘**Background Note 2.8,** which provides information about television advertising in political campaigns. Ask: **Why do you think a political campaign might be willing to pay for media time to convey its** own messages to the public? *(By controlling the content the public receives, the campaign can create positive images about its own candidate—or negative ones about its opponent.)* Ask students to describe any campaign ads they may be familiar with and discuss whether they think the ad is effective and why.

2. Introduce the Lesson There are a wealth of Web sites that provide ads from various presidential campaigns. Have students peruse one or more of these sites in class or for homework, or explore them as a class. You may wish to direct students to find and view some specific campaign ads, such as Lyndon Johnson's famous "Daisy" ad, the cheerful "I Like Ike" ads, or Reagan's "Morning in America" campaign, as well as recent ads. Discuss with students what qualities they think made the commercials effective or controversial. Ask: **Do you think a television commercial will always help a candidate? How might a commercial cause harm to a political campaign?**

3. Complete the Activity Distribute ✒**Activity 2.8,** *Television Commercial Script,* in which students write a script for a television commercial for a candidate for office. To help them in their preparations, provide students with copies of the candidate profiles and state profiles that they created in earlier lessons. Make sure students recognize that their commercial should promote their candidate and present a positive message.

Instruct students to first consider what kind of ad they want. For example, the ad could be a dramatization, such as a family talking about a public policy issue. Or the ad could feature the candidate or a narrator speaking to listeners. Students should provide a brief description of their ad as well as a script. The ad should be timed so that it lasts no longer than 30 seconds.

> **L2 Differentiate** Have students dictate their commercial into a recording device.

> **L2 ELL Differentiate** Have students write their commercial initially in their first language, and then have them translate the ad into English.

4. Debrief When students have completed the activity, have each student give a reading of his or her script to the class. Tell students to offer their constructive criticisms of each ad—what parts worked and what parts did not. Ask: **Do you think one of these advertisement could influence your vote? Why or why not?**

5. Assess Distribute ✒**Assessment 2.8,** in which students answer questions that explore what they have learned about paid media.

EXTEND THE LESSON

> **L3 Differentiate** Have the class divide the various ads that their classmates have written into the following categories: positive, comparative, and negative. Then ask volunteers to explain to the rest of the class what kind of ad they think works best in what kinds of situations and why.

TEACHER INSTRUCTIONS

PURPOSE

To frame an answer to the ❧ **Essential Question,** *In what ways should people participate in public affairs?,* students should understand that money—collecting it and spending it—is a key factor in our political system. Informed citizens need to understand that money is both a cause for concern and a vehicle for participation in politics.

LESSON GOALS

- Explain the ways that money is raised and spent in a typical political campaign.
- Debate the benefits and drawbacks of placing limits on political donations and spending.

MATERIALS

- ⊘**Online Student Edition** and copies of **Background Notes 2.9A** and **2.9B,** located at PearsonSuccessNet.com
- *Essential Questions Journal*
- ⊘Copies of **Activity 2.9,** *Money and Politics Pro and Con,* located at PearsonSuccessNet.com
- ⊘Copies of **Assessment 2.9,** located at PearsonSuccessNet.com

BEFORE CLASS

Distribute copies of ⊘**Background Notes 2.9A** and **2.9B.** For more in-depth information, refer students to the ⊘**Online Student Edition** Chapter 9, Sections 1 and 3. You may wish to have students read these materials before coming to class. You may also want students to complete the *Essential Questions Journal* Chapter 9 Warmup Essay, p. 74, and Explorations 1 and 3, pp. 75 and 77, before class.

> **L2 Differentiate** Pair students to create graphic organizers of the main ideas and supporting details in each Background Note.

> **L2 Differentiate** Have students listen to the audio summary available at PearsonSuccessNet.com

TEACH

1. Build Background Review what students have learned about paid media and its importance in many political campaigns. Explain that television advertising can be very expensive. In fact, television advertising is one of the major expenses in today's very costly elections. Ask: **Where do you think candidates get the money they need to carry out their campaigns?** *(Examples: individual donors, business interests, and political parties and special interest groups that raise money for political purposes.)* Review ⊘**Background Note 2.9A,** which provides information about interest groups and their Political Action Committees. Ask: **Describe the tension that exists over the creation of interest groups and their influence on politics.** *(Being part of interest groups is a*

UNIT 2

LESSON

9

Money and Politics

good way to take part in public affairs. But undue influence of interest groups may at times seem or even be undemocratic.)

2. Introduce the Lesson Explain that concern over the influence of special interests—and especially, money—has led to efforts to control how candidates for office collect and spend money. Review ⓐ**Background Note 2.9B,** which explores the history of campaign finance reform. Tell students that reform efforts have raised questions about how to maintain the integrity of the electoral process while at the same time honoring the right of individuals to take part in public affairs by making monetary contributions to campaigns and interest groups.

3. Complete the Activity Distribute ⓐ**Activity Sheet 2.9.** Have students use their knowledge of campaign financing and campaign finance reform to identify arguments for and against regulation of each item mentioned.

> **L2 Differentiate** Assist students by explaining the meaning of difficult terms listed on the activity sheet. For example, *PAC* means "political action committee," and it is a political arm of a special interest group. *Corporate* refers to business and companies that might give money to a campaign. *Soft money* is money given to party organizations or groups not connected to a campaign.

4. Debrief When students have completed the activity, have volunteers share their pro and con answers with the class. Ask students to respond to the answers their classmates provide. Then ask students to think about how different parts of our political culture may have different points of view about these questions. Ask: **Do you think the point of view of a candidate or someone who is working on a political campaign may differ from that of an ordinary citizen?** *(The candidate or campaigner is more likely to want to have access to money, while an ordinary citizen may prefer that all candidates have a level financial playing field.)* Then ask: **Do you think you should be free to reward or support those candidates you favor with financial help?** *(Students may feel that that is a valid use of their money.)* **Do you think candidates who are able to attract more financial support deserve whatever advantage they can obtain?** *(Students may say that a candidate may be able to obtain money not only by having popular views, but also by being willing to do what wealthy supporters want, and that's where the danger lies.)*

5. Assess Distribute ⓐ**Assessment 2.9,** in which students answer a series of questions that explore what they have learned about the role of money in politics.

EXTEND THE LESSON ▬▬▬▬▬▬▬▬▬

> **L3 Differentiate** Have students write a newspaper editorial in which they address the tension between the need to allow freedom of expression and the need to protect the integrity of the political process. Ask them to read at least 3 editorials from print or online newspapers, and discuss the characteristics of an editorial before they begin.

UNIT 2

LESSON 10

Political Campaign

PURPOSE

To help frame an answer to the 🔑 **Essential Question,** *In what ways should people participate in public affairs?,* students will conduct a mock Political Campaign for one of two candidates.

LESSON GOALS

- Apply knowledge about elections, voter behavior, the media, and interest groups to conduct a simulated political campaign.
- Evaluate information, produce several pieces of campaign literature, and take part in a staged media event.
- Appreciate and explain the value of civic participation.

MATERIALS

- Copies of 🅐**Activity 2.10A,** *Acceptance Speech,* located at PearsonSuccessNet.com
- Copies of 🅐**Activity 2.10B,** *Plan an Advertising Campaign,* located at PearsonSuccessNet.com
- Copies of 🅐**Activity 2.10C,** *Debate Preparation,* located at PearsonSuccessNet.com
- **Campaign 2.a—*Candidate A Profile***
- **Campaign 2.b—*Candidate B Profile***
- **Campaign 2.c—*District Map and Profile***
- **Campaign 2.d—*Polling Results***
- **Campaign 2.e—*Newspaper Article***

BEFORE CLASS

Have students review the activities from the unit, including the press release they wrote as part of Lesson 6 and the campaign commercial they wrote as part of Lesson 8. Have students read these materials before Day 1 of the simulation.

TEACH

Introduce the Lesson Remind students of the **Unit 2** 🔑 **Essential Question:** *In what ways should people participate in public affairs?* Explain that a major avenue for this participation is elections and the many activities associated with them. Review with students what they have explored over the past several days: the processes for voting and nominating candidates, the factors that influence and help predict voter behavior, the role of the media—how it is used and how it affects elections—and the role of interest groups and money in elections. Present students with the following prompt: Explain how electoral politics allows citizens several different ways to take part in public affairs. *(Elections allow citizens to vote, and they provide a great occasion for them to become informed. They also give people an opportunity to participate in civic life directly, and to understand how the media and other factors affect their views.)*

DAY 1

1. Introduce the Candidates Have student volunteers read aloud the candidate profiles contained in **Campaign 2.a** and **2.b.** Explain that the two candidates profiled will be competing in an election in which students will play key roles, drawing upon their knowledge of voters, voter behavior, and the media.

2. Explore the District Ask a student volunteer to read aloud **Campaign 2.c,** which contains data about the district in which this election will be taking place. Have volunteers summarize the information about the district as it is relevant to a political campaign. Prompt as needed. For example, what are the district's main occupations and how do they suggest voters' main concerns? Then ask students to brainstorm 3–5 national, international, or local issues. Write these issues on the board and have students assign a percentage of the district's voters as agreeing or disagreeing. Sample issues: bringing home troops from abroad, government regulation for environmental protection, less regulation of local development, lower taxes, funds for a new high school.

3. Assign Roles Divide the class in half, with each half taking responsibility for the campaign of one of the two candidates. Within each half, you can further divide the class into smaller groups of 3–5 students of differing ability levels.

4. Assign Speech Activity Distribute ⊘**Activity 2.10A,** *Acceptance Speech,* in which students work in their teams to draft a speech for their candidate.

5. Conclude Tell students that on Day 2, they will engage in activities involving the media.

DAY 2

1. Team Activities Divide the class again into their campaign teams. Have each team work independently on one of the following two activities for 15 minutes or so. Then have teams switch to the other activity.

Part I *Advertising Activity* Distribute to one team ⊘**Activity 2.10B,** *Plan an Advertising Campaign.* Then distribute **Campaign 2.d,** *Polling Results,* which shows the results of recent polling on some issues affecting the campaign. Give team members a few moments to review the information. Have students use the information from **Campaign 2.d** to help them identify and plan out their campaign advertising.

Part II *News Story Activity* To the other campaign team, distribute **Campaign 2.e,** *Newspaper Article.* Have a volunteer read the news story aloud. Explain that this event was unplanned but that the public is looking to the campaign to issue a press release about the incident. Have students work in teams to produce a press release in response to the story. The press release should clearly indicate their candidate's views on the events and on the larger issues that the incident involves. Remind students that they can review **Activity 2.6A,** *Sample Press Release,* as well as **Activity 2.6B,** *Writing a Press Release.*

2. Debate Prep Activity Arrange students again in their campaign teams. Distribute ⊘**Activity 2.10C,** *Debate Preparation,* in which students prepare a list of questions for their candidate's opponent for use in an upcoming debate. Before students begin, ask them to recall what they have learned about their candidate, their opponent, the district, and its voters. Have students also think about the role of media in campaigns. Ask: **What makes a television debate such a significant event in a political campaign?** (*Many voters rely heavily on television for their information about public affairs. It is a major influence on public opinion.*)

After teams have written their debate questions, have them exchange their lists with their opponents. Then have teams spend some time formulating possible answers to the debate questions. As teams work on their answers, remind them to keep in mind that this debate will be televised. Ask: **How might the medium of television affect the way they have their candidate answer questions?** (*It is important on television to be clear, brief, and to the point. Answers that are long and involved may go over viewers' heads. In addition, candidates will need to maintain the appearance of calm and control. It is the image as much as the content that matters in television.*) Have teams volunteer to read their questions and sample answers to the class. Invite the class to offer constructive criticism of the answers. Explore together how a television audience might perceive answers.

DAY 3

1. Debrief Conduct a post-campaign debriefing. Review with students the different activities they have engaged in during the simulation.

- As a citizen and future voter, what did you gain from **Activity 2.10A** writing an acceptance speech on Day 1 of the simulation? What did you learn about the way a candidate's speech reflects individual views but also the characteristics of voters?

- How did **Activity 2.10B,** the advertising campaign activity, influence your understanding of the role of media in political campaigns? How might you view campaign commercials differently as a result of having taken part in this activity?

- How did the news story about the immigration raid change the campaign?

- How did **Activity 2.10.C** affect your view of televised debates?

- How might you, as a citizen and future voter, change your involvement in the political process as a result of this simulation?

2. Assess Have students answer the 🌐 **Essential Question:** *In what ways should people participate in public affairs?*, in their *Essential Questions Journal.* You may also use one of the following formats:

- Write an essay.
- Present the answer in a multimedia format.
- Present the answer in a visual format.
- Create a skit that shows various ways that people can participate in public affairs.

EXTEND THE LESSON

L3 Differentiate Have students research some of the issues raised during this campaign and engage in an actual campaign debate. Assign students the roles of candidates and moderator, and invite the rest of the class to judge the debate performance. You may wish to record the debates and play back the recordings for students to critique.

L4 Differentiate Have students actually produce the advertising campaign that they planned on Day 2 of the simulation. Ask them to add Web sites, e-mail blasts, text messaging, and Twittering to their plan.

UNIT OVERVIEW

This group of lessons focuses on Congress, including its structure and functions, its powers, the meaning of representation, and the lawmaking process. The lessons culminate in a classroom Mock Congress. At the end of this unit, students will be able to craft an answer to the 🌐 **Essential Question: *What makes a successful Congress?*** You may wish to have students begin their study by completing the ***Essential Questions Journal*** Unit 3 Warmup, p. 77.

UNIT GOALS

- Compare different views of representation.
- Describe the structure and functions of Congress.
- Explain congressional powers and understand debates over the interpretation of these powers.
- Understand the complexity of the legislative process and the factors that enter into legislators' decision making.
- Evaluate the questions of what makes a successful Congress and how the lawmaking process might be improved.

TIME ALLOTMENT

This unit of activities is intended to be taught in 10 days (or 5 days on a block schedule).

DAY 1	Lesson 1	Representatives and Representation
DAY 2	Lesson 2	Interactive Decision Making: How Should Members of Congress Vote?
DAY 3	Lesson 3	Congressional Powers
DAY 4	Lesson 4	Getting to Congress: Elections and Districts
DAY 5	Lesson 5	Organization of Congress
DAY 6	Lesson 6	Committees and Committee Assignments
DAY 7	Lesson 7	Bills and How They Become Law
DAY 8	Lesson 8	The Committees Meet
DAY 9	Lesson 9	Mock Congress
DAY 10	Lesson 10	Wrap-Up

ENDURING UNDERSTANDINGS

- Members of Congress must balance roles as local, state, and national leaders.
- The organizational structure of Congress allows it to do an enormous quantity of work.
- The powers of Congress have been interpreted increasingly broadly, despite ongoing debate over appropriate limits on those powers.
- The meaning of the expressed powers is found as much in the ways in which these powers have been carried out as in the words of the Constitution.
- The lawmaking process is complex, requiring both organizational skills and compromise.

UNIT 3

LESSON 1

Representatives and Representation

TEACHER INSTRUCTIONS

PURPOSE
To help frame an answer to the ❦ **Essential Question:** *What makes a successful Congress?*, students need to understand the nature of representation, which requires members of Congress to act as both national leaders and representatives of their constituents.

LESSON GOALS
- Define *representation*.
- Identify the historical reasons for a bicameral Congress.
- Explain the ways in which members of Congress may represent their constituents.

MATERIALS
- ⦿ **Online Student Edition** and copies of ⦿ **Background Notes 3.1A** and **3.1B,** located at PearsonSuccessNet.com
- *Essential Questions Journal*
- Copies of ⦿ **Activity 3.1,** *What Is Representation?,* located at PearsonSuccessNet.com
- Copies of ⦿ **Assessment 3.1,** located at PearsonSuccessNet.com
- Internet access

BEFORE CLASS
Distribute copies of ⦿ **Background Notes 3.1A** and **3.1B.** For more in-depth information, refer students to the ⦿ **Online Student Edition** Chapter 10, Sections 1 and 4. You may wish to have students read these materials before coming to class. You may also wish to have students complete the *Essential Questions Journal* Chapter 10 Warmup, p. 78, and Chapter 10 Exploration, Parts I and II, pp. 79–80, before class.

> **L2 Differentiate** Instead of students reading the Background Notes on their own, have volunteers take turns reading portions of them aloud in class. After each portion is read, have a volunteer other than the reader summarize the information.

> **L2 Differentiate** Have students listen to the audio summary located at PearsonSuccessNet.com.

TEACH

1. Activate Prior Knowledge Tell students that the goal of this unit is to explore the ❦ **Essential Question:** *What makes a successful Congress?* To help them start thinking about this question, have them take out the *Essential Questions Journal* Unit Warmup, p. 77, where they identified criteria for judging a successful Congress, or have them complete the assignment in class. Take a poll and record on a poster how many students chose each option. Tell students to keep these ideas in mind as they study this unit. Display this poster for the duration of the unit and return to it when discussing the 🌐 **Essential Question** at the end of the unit.

2. Introduce the Lesson Tell students that, although there are various ways to judge the success of Congress, many people judge the success of their individual members of Congress by how much those members do for their constituents. For example, members of Congress may support legislation that includes funding for local roads or a state history museum. Present the class with a map of your state showing its towns and congressional districts. Ask: **What is representation? How many representatives does your local district have in Congress?** Lead a discussion to find out how much they already know about their members of Congress and about what members of Congress do. Also review the historical reasons for a bicameral legislature and the views of representation discussed in the Background Notes.

3. Complete the Activity Ask: **Who do members of Congress represent?** List ideas on the board. Then ask: **Do members of Congress represent the nation? All the people in your state or district? The people who voted for them? Their campaign contributors? Their party? Their own views and interests? A combination?** Explain that members of Congress have differing ideas about representation. Lead a discussion about what difference it might make who a member of Congress believes he or she represents. Who would students want their own members of Congress to represent? Explain that students, working in groups, will now spend twenty minutes researching the Web sites of their representatives and senators to determine what issues and initiatives they emphasize and to make inferences about which groups members of Congress see as their major constituencies.

> **L2 Differentiate ELL** If research would be too time-consuming, present pages from your district's House representative's Web site and fill in the activity sheet as a class. Write key terms on the board and ask for definitions: *Congress, constituent/constituency, representative.*

4. Debrief Ask students to reflect as a class on what they have found by sharing their ideas. What issues were highlighted on representatives' and senators' Web sites? What clues can they find to tell which constituent groups members of Congress are most concerned about? When the students have differing views of the information they analyzed, encourage them to use evidence from the Web sites to argue for their interpretations.

5. Assess Distribute 📄**Assessment 3.1,** which asks students to consider a scenario and how a senator should vote.

EXTEND THE LESSON

> **L3 Differentiate** Have students complete *Apply What You've Learned* in the 📄**Online Student Edition** Chapter 10 Assessment, and the **Essential Questions Journal** Chapter 10 *Apply What You've Learned* Activity, p. 82.

> **L4 Differentiate** Have students research the campaign donations to one of their senators. Ask them if they see a correlation between the senator's votes and the people who donated large amounts of money.

UNIT 3

LESSON 2

TEACHER INSTRUCTIONS

PURPOSE

To frame an answer to the question: *Whose views should members of Congress represent when voting?*, students will take on the role of a member of Congress making a decision about how to vote on a controversial bill.

LESSON GOALS

- Experience and describe the challenges members of Congress face when voting.
- Decide how to vote on a controversial bill.

MATERIALS

- **Online Interactive Decision Making,** located at PearsonSuccessNet.com
- *Essential Questions Journal*

BEFORE CLASS

Refer students to the **Online Student Edition** Chapter 10, Section 4. You may wish to have students read this material before coming to class. You may also want students to review the *Essential Questions Journal* Chapter 10 Warmup, p. 78, and Exploration, pp. 80, before class.

TEACH

1. Introduce the Lesson Tell students that members of Congress represent their constituents, but that is more difficult than it sounds. Explain that, today, they will make a decision about how they would vote on a controversial bill.

2. Complete the Activity Have students complete the online activity in class or assign the simulation as homework. NOTE: If you decide to give this as a homework assignment, conduct the Debrief at the beginning of class and then continue with the next day's lesson plan described on the following page.

3. Debrief Once students have completed the online simulation, lead a discussion about how members of Congress should vote. Ask: **Whose opinions should matter when a member of Congress casts a vote?** *(Answers may include the legislator's opinion, the majority of constituents, influential constituents, lobbyists, experts in various fields, and party leaders.)* **What pieces of information did you rank as most important in the simulation? Why?** *(Answers will vary.)* Use students' answers to identify the models of representation *(trustee, partisan, delegate, politico).*

4. Assess Have students rank the most important considerations for members of Congress when they vote and follow up with a discussion of how the interactivity helps provide an answer to the question: *Whose views should members of Congress represent when voting?* You may also want to have students complete the Chapter 10 Essential Question Essay on p. 83 in their *Essential Questions Journal.*

TEACHER INSTRUCTIONS

PURPOSE

To help frame an answer to the 🌎 **Essential Question:** *What makes a successful Congress?,* students need to understand what powers are granted to Congress and how members of Congress make decisions.

LESSON GOALS

- List and describe the expressed powers of Congress.
- Explain the debate over the limits on the implied powers.
- Describe how the commerce power has allowed Congress to expand its powers.

MATERIALS

- ⏺**Online Student Edition** and copies of ⏺**Background Note 3.3,** located at PearsonSuccessNet.com
- *Essential Questions Journal*
- Copies of ⏺**Activity 3.3A,** *Powers of Congress,* and ⏺**Activity 3.3B,** *Implied Powers of Congress,* located at PearsonSuccessNet.com
- Copies of ⏺**Assessment 3.3,** located at PearsonSuccessNet.com

BEFORE CLASS

Distribute copies of ⏺**Background Note 3.3.** For more in-depth information, refer students to the ⏺**Online Student Edition,** Chapter 11. You may wish to have students read these materials before coming to class. You may also wish to have students complete the *Essential Questions Journal* Chapter 11 Warmup, p. 84, and Exploration, Parts II and III, pp. 86–87, before class.

> **L2 Differentiate** Ask students to write down 3–5 main ideas from the Background Note, exchange them with a partner, and agree on three main points to share with the class. Write these points on the board and help students select those that create the most accurate summary.

> **L2 Differentiate** Have students listen to the audio summary located at PearsonSuccessNet.com.

TEACH

1. Activate Prior Knowledge In a class brainstorm, list actions from students' daily routine. Record these on the board and identify actions that have been affected by federal laws. For example, the Food and Drug Administration regulates food and medication, and federal funds support many regional highway projects. Explain to students that the Constitution gives Congress specific expressed powers, but over time congressional power has expanded beyond what the Framers could have imagined.

2. Introduce the Lesson Refer students to *The Expressed Powers of Congress: Why These Powers?* on p. 305 of the ⦿**Online Student Edition**. Tell students that Congress has specific, enumerated powers granted by the Constitution and that James Madison laid out the powers and reasons for them in *The Federalist Papers*. Ask volunteers to read each piece of the feature aloud.

3. Complete the Activities Distribute ⦿**Activity 3.3A,** *Powers of Congress.* In the chart, students will identify where each power of Congress is found in the Constitution. With a partner, have them use the Background Note, online textbook, and the Constitution (available in the online textbook) to identify limits on each power. Have students review the list of ways in which federal laws affect their lives on the board. Have volunteers circle reflections of the expressed powers on the board. It is likely that few of the actions and laws on the board stem from the expressed powers. Ask students how Congress has been able to make all these laws. Use the discussion to introduce the Necessary and Proper Clause and discuss the expansion of power based on the Commerce Clause. Distribute ⦿**Activity 3.3B,** *Implied Powers of Congress,* and have students identify the expressed power that gave Congress the power to act in each scenario. They will then evaluate the constitutionality of each action.

4. Debrief Review students' evaluations of the constitutionality of each congressional action. Remind them that they will be writing their own bills as part of the Mock Congress activity at the end of this unit of study, and that they will need to evaluate their own bills to be sure they fall within the powers of Congress. Then discuss ⦿**Background Note 3.3** and the ongoing debate over implied powers.

5. Assess Distribute ⦿**Assessment 3.3,** which asks students to identify the three most important powers of Congress and justify their choices.

EXTEND THE LESSON

L4 Differentiate Ask students to extend the chart in ⦿**Activity 3.3A** by using the Constitution to identify the other enumerated powers.

L3 Differentiate Have students research *McCulloch* v. *Maryland,* either online or in the ⦿**Online Student Edition.** Ask them to summarize each side's argument in the case and the Court's decision.

TEACHER INSTRUCTIONS

PURPOSE

To help frame an answer to the ❧ **Essential Question:** *What makes a successful congress?*, students need to understand how members of Congress are elected.

LESSON GOALS

- Describe congressional elections.
- Explain the process of gerrymandering and the controversy surrounding it.

MATERIALS

- ⊘ **Online Student Edition** and copies of ⊘ **Background Notes 3.4A** and **3.4B,** located at PearsonSuccessNet.com
- *Essential Questions Journal*
- Copies of ⊘ **Activity 3.4,** *Gerrymandering,* located at PearsonSuccessNet.com
- Copies of ⊘ **Assessment 3.4,** located at PearsonSuccessNet.com
- Map of your state showing congressional districts

BEFORE CLASS

Distribute copies of ⊘ **Background Notes 3.4A** and **3.4B.** For more in-depth information, refer students to the ⊘ **Online Student Edition** Chapter 10, Sections 2 and 3 and Chapter 12, Section 1. You may wish to have students read these materials before coming to class. You may also wish to have students complete the *Essential Questions Journal* Chapter 10 Exploration, Part III, p. 81, and Chapter 12 Exploration, Part I, p. 91, before class.

> **L2 Differentiate** Before students read ⊘ **Background Note 3.4B,** ask them to look at the graphic description of gerrymandering on pp. 276–277 of the ⊘ **Online Student Edition** and review it as a class.

> **L2 Differentiate** Have students listen to the audio summary located at PearsonSuccessNet.com.

TEACH

1. Activate Prior Knowledge Display a map of your state's congressional districts. Ask students which members represent them in Congress and in which congressional district students reside. (They should name their representative and senators.) Ask them to describe their congressional district. Then ask them to explain how the roles of their representative and their senators differ. Emphasize that senators represent a whole state, while most representatives are elected from a smaller district. Ask if students know how district lines are drawn for congressional districts and what the differences in qualifications for senators and representatives are. Explain that today they will learn more about these topics.

2. Discuss Using the Background Notes and 🟢 **Online Student Edition,** have students look up and list the formal requirements for election to the Senate and the House. Record these on the board. As a class, discuss whether students think that these requirements are sufficient prerequisites for election. Brainstorm a list of other attributes students would like their senators and representatives to have. You may also choose to discuss other differences between senators and members of the house, including the length of terms and relative power of each position.

3. Complete the Activity Explain that the districting system makes the House and Senate very different. States are divided into districts of roughly equal population that elect one representative each. In only seven states do senators represent the same constituency as representatives. The district lines, or the processes for drawing them, are established by state legislatures. Explain that "gerrymandering" is when state legislators draw districts for partisan reasons. Distribute 🟢 **Activity 3.4,** which asks students to draw district lines. Assign one third of the class to Party X, one third to Party Y, and one third to the election commission. Allow students to work alone or in pairs with another student assigned to the same group.

4. Debrief After students draw their district lines, invite volunteers from each of the three groupings to draw their district lines on the board. Discuss their divisions and use the examples to identify "packing" and "cracking." Then discuss the Reflection Questions.

5. Assess Distribute 🟢 **Assessment 3.4,** which asks students about qualifications for members of Congress and the redistricting process.

EXTEND THE LESSON ▬▬▬▬▬▬▬▬▬▬▬▬▬▬▬▬▬▬▬

L3 Differentiate Have students investigate how district lines are drawn in their state and evaluate the current districts to identify oddly shaped districts that may have been gerrymandered.

TEACHER INSTRUCTIONS

PURPOSE

To help frame an answer to the 🌐 Essential Question: *What makes a successful Congress?,* students need to understand how Congress is organized and how that organization helps Congress do its work. They also need to consider the reasons for such an organizational structure and how Congress should balance efficiency and democracy.

LESSON GOALS

- Describe the organizational structure of Congress.
- Identify the constitutional and party officers in Congress and explain their roles.
- Explain the seniority system.

MATERIALS

- 🖉 Online Student Edition and copies of 🖉 Background Notes 3.5A and 3.5B, located at PearsonSuccessNet.com
- *Essential Questions Journal*
- Copies of 🖉 Activity 3.5, *Organization of Congress,* located at PearsonSuccessNet.com
- Copies of 🖉 Assessment 3.5, located at PearsonSuccessNet.com
- Internet access

BEFORE CLASS

Distribute copies of 🖉 Background Notes 3.5A and 3.5B. For more in-depth information, refer students to the 🖉 Online Student Edition Chapter 12, Sections 1 and 2. You may wish to have students read these materials before coming to class. You may also wish to have students complete the *Essential Questions Journal* Chapter 12 Exploration, Part I, p. 91, before class.

> **L2 Differentiate** Ask students to write down 3–5 main ideas from the Background Notes, exchange them with a partner, and agree on three main points to share with the class. Write these points on the board and help students select those that create the most accurate summary.

> **L2 Differentiate** Have students listen to the audio summary located at PearsonSuccessNet.com.

TEACH

1. Activate Prior Knowledge In a class brainstorm, ask students to volunteer information about how Congress is organized, including naming leadership positions and current leaders. Take notes on the board and use these to evaluate students' background knowledge and guide discussion throughout the lesson. Use the opportunity to clarify any misconceptions students may have.

2. Introduce the Lesson Explain that Congress has grown from a very small group to its current size—100 senators and 435 representatives. It deals with thousands of individual bills in each session. You may wish to display Transparency 12F, which shows the number of bills that are introduced in each session of Congress, the numbers that are reported from committees, and the numbers that become law. Ask students to envision what types of challenges Congress might face because of its size and amount of work and to speculate on solutions that Congress evolved over time. Ask what type of leaders might be needed to get work done. Explain to the students that Congress has developed an organizational structure that includes leadership positions described in the Constitution and party leadership positions, which are not established by the Constitution.

3. Complete the Activity Distribute ✷**Activity 3.5,** which asks students to explain each of the leadership roles in Congress and identify the people who currently hold each position. Students will need access to the Internet or ✷**Online Student Edition** to complete the activity.

4. Debrief Review students' answers to the activity sheet. Ask students what they notice about the election dates of the leaders. *(All the leaders have been in Congress for a long time.)* Ask for a simple explanation of the seniority system and ask what students think about it. Ask: **Should all members of Congress have equal power? What type of power does a brand-new member hold? Should longevity be rewarded? Why or why not?** Ask students to make predictions about how a powerful member of Congress might be able to influence legislation. Ask: **Is the distribution of power fair to those Americans who are represented by less-powerful members of Congress?**

5. Assess Distribute ✷**Assessment 3.5,** which asks students to further consider issues related to organization and seniority.

EXTEND THE LESSON ▬▬▬▬▬▬▬▬▬▬▬▬▬▬▬▬▬▬▬▬▬▬▬

L4 Differentiate Have students use the Internet to find information about each party's caucus and the procedures for selecting party leaders. Then have them summarize this information in a poster.

L3 Differentiate Have students use the Internet to research the Web sites of the minority and majority leaders in the House and Senate. Using this information, students should summarize the legislative and organizational support that the party leadership provides for members.

TEACHER INSTRUCTIONS

PURPOSE

To help frame an answer to the 🎯 **Essential Question:** *What makes a successful Congress?*, students need to understand how committees help Congress to do its work.

LESSON GOALS

- Introduce the steps of the legislative process by watching a video.
- Establish the importance of committees in the legislative process.
- Explain what committees do.
- Describe the jurisdiction of each committee in the House.

MATERIALS

- 📀 **Online Student Edition** and copies of 📀 **Background Note 3.6,** located at PearsonSuccessNet.com
- *Essential Questions Journal*
- *American Government Essential Questions Video* DVD or 📀 online at PearsonSuccessNet.com
- Copies of 📀 **Activity 3.6,** *Committees in Congress,* located at PearsonSuccessNet.com
- Copies of 📀 **Assessment 3.6,** located at PearsonSuccessNet.com

BEFORE CLASS

Refer students to the 📀 **Online Student Edition** Chapter 12, Section 2 and distribute copies of 📀 **Background Note 3.6.** You may wish to have students read these materials before coming to class. For more in-depth information, refer students to the 📀 **Online Student Edition** Chapter 10, Section 4. You may also wish to have students complete the *Essential Questions Journal* Chapter 12 Exploration, Part II, pp. 92–93, before class.

> **L2 Differentiate** Instead of students reading the Background Note on their own, have volunteers take turns reading portions aloud in class. After each portion is read, have a volunteer other than the reader summarize the information.

> **L2 Differentiate** Have students listen to the audio summary located at PearsonSuccessNet.com.

TEACH

1. Activate Prior Knowledge Ask students if they have ever planned for a large event, such as a sports tournament, a play, or a school dance. If they have, ask how many people were involved in the planning. Was it one person or a group? Use their answers to guide a discussion about the division of labor. Draw parallels between congressional committees and other committees, which exist to divide work that would be too much for one person or one group.

2. Introduce the Lesson Tell students that today they are going to learn about committees in Congress. This information will help them with the role they will play in the Mock Congress activity at the end of Unit 3, in which each student will be assigned to a committee to consider bills. Show the Unit 3 *American Government Essential Questions Video,* which introduces the process of how a bill becomes a law. Discuss the process, emphasizing that the sheer number of bills submitted is too great for all members to debate each one. Explain that the large majority of bills die in committees.

> **L2 Differentiate** Ask students to look up and define *standing committees, select committees, joint committees,* and *conference committees.* Make sure students understand that they will be addressing the standing committees in the activity.

3. Complete the Activity Divide students into pairs or groups of three and direct them to the ⨀Online Student Edition and ⨀Background Note 3.6. Using these resources, have them make a flowchart that begins with "Speaker refers a bill to committee." The flowchart should show what happens to a bill in committee and the actions that a committee may take related to a bill. When students finish, review the process as a class to check for understanding. Explain that there are 20 committees in the House of Representatives, each with its own jurisdiction, or area of expertise. Distribute ⨀Activity 3.6 and have students match the committee name with its jurisdiction.

4. Debrief Review the answers to ⨀Activity 3.6 and answer any questions students may have. Ask students how committees in the House compare to committees in the Senate. Ask: **Is the committee system is the best way to be sure that good bills will be passed? What are some of the pitfalls of the committee system?**

5. Assess Distribute ⨀Assessment 3.6, which asks students to read several scenarios and identify which standing committee would review the bills described.

EXTEND THE LESSON ▬▬▬▬▬▬▬▬▬▬▬▬▬▬▬▬▬

> **L3 Differentiate** Assign groups of students one congressional committee. Have them create a poster that explains the jurisdiction of each committee, its history, its chairperson, and its ranking member.

> **L4 Differentiate** Have students choose a committee in either house of Congress. Ask them to investigate the majority and minority Web sites for that committee and analyze the ways in which the views of the parties compare on policy areas addressed by the committee.

TEACHER INSTRUCTIONS

PURPOSE

To help frame an answer to the 🏛 **Essential Question:** *What makes a successful Congress?,* students need to understand how a bill becomes a law.

LESSON GOALS

- Trace the path of a bill through the lawmaking process.
- Identify the source of bills submitted to Congress.
- Write a bill.

MATERIALS

- ❼**Online Student Edition** and copies of ❼**Background Notes 3.7A** and **3.7B**, located at PearsonSuccessNet.com
- *Essential Questions Journal*
- **Congress 3.a:** *How a Bill Becomes a Law* poster
- **Congress 3.b:** *Ethanol brochure*
- **Congress 3.c:** *New York Times* editorial
- **Congress 3.d:** *Memo from congressional staffer*
- **Congress 3.e:** *Representative's Web site*
- Copies of ❼**Activity 3.7A,** *How to Write a Bill,* and ❼**Activity 3.7B,** *Write a Bill,* located at PearsonSuccessNet.com
- Copies of ❼**Assessment 3.7**
- Internet access

BEFORE CLASS

Distribute copies of ❼**Background Notes 3.7A** and **3.7B**. For more in-depth information, refer students to the ❼**Online Student Edition** Chapter 12, Sections 3 and 4. You may wish to have students read these materials before coming to class. You may also wish to have students complete the *Essential Questions Journal* Chapter 12 Warmup, p. 90, and Chapter 12 Exploration, Parts III and IV, pp. 94–95, before class.

> **L2 Differentiate** Have students listen to the audio summary located at PearsonSuccessNet.com.

TEACH

1. Introduce the Lesson Tell students that during this lesson they will learn the steps of how a bill becomes a law and then draft their own bills. Display **Congress 3.a,** a poster that explains how a bill becomes a law. Have students read each step aloud and discuss students' questions. Ask: **How would this chart be different if a bill were first introduced in the Senate? How would it be different if similar bills were introduced in both houses simultaneously?**

2. Brainstorm Ask students where bills may originate and how legislators decide which bills to support. Write students' ideas on the board. Ideas for bills may come from legislators themselves, interest groups, constituents, the executive branch, or even from within committees. Legislators may consider their own views, those of their party, and those of their constituents in deciding how to act on a bill. Introduce **Congress 3.b,** a brochure promoting ethanol (example of an interest group that may contribute to writing a bill). Explain that interest groups often take part in writing bills. The second step of the lawmaking process is for lawmakers to gather information about bills on which they will have to vote. Introduce **Congress 3.c,** a *New York Times* editorial supporting nuclear power, which provides an example of public input on an issue, and **Congress 3.d,** a memo advising a member of Congress, which is an example of the type of information a member of Congress may seek out. Then introduce **Congress 3.e,** a representative's Web site explaining her position. Explain that this is an example of how a member of Congress may convey a policy stance to constituents.

3. Prepare to Write Bills Divide students into pairs or triads and distribute ⊘**Activities 3.7A and 3.7B.** Tell students that the materials just introduced are all related to energy and environmental issues. They may write a bill about one of these topics using data provided, or they may write a bill about another topic of their choosing.

> **L2 Differentiate** Suggest that students pick up a topic and wording for a bill from either **Congress 3.b** or **Congress 3.d.**

4. Review Sample Bill Refer students to ⊘**Background Note 3.7B,** a sample bill. This bill was submitted in the Senate during the 110th Congress and referred to the Committee on Energy and Natural Resources. Ask students to use the description of the parts of a bill on ⊘**Activity 3.7A** to identify each part of the sample bill. Students should note the formal language used in the bill and try to emulate it when they write their own bills.

5. Complete the Activity Have students follow the directions for ⊘**Activities 3.7A** and **3.7B,** and review **Congress 3.b, 3.c, 3.d,** and **3.e** to learn about energy and environmental issues. (Alternatively, you may choose to have students do Internet research if they have chosen their own topic.) Then have them use the directions on the activity sheet to write a bill.

> **L3 Differentiate** For a shorter activity, allow students to use only the information provided on **Congress 3.b, Congress 3.c., Congress 3.d,** and **Congress 3.e** to write their bills.

6. Submit Bills When students finish their bills, they will submit them to the "Speaker" (teacher) for referral to a committee. This will happen in the next class period.

> **L3 Differentiate** Make a "hopper" and have students submit bills in the box.

7. Assess Distribute ⊘**Assessment 3.7,** which asks students to identify where a bill can die.

EXTEND THE LESSON

> **L3 Differentiate** Have students find a bill at thomas.loc.gov and follow the path of that bill through Congress.

TEACHER INSTRUCTIONS

PURPOSE

To help frame an answer to the ✪ Essential Question: *What makes a successful Congress?*, students will meet as members of a committee to discuss bills as committee members and servants of their constituents.

LESSON GOALS

- Learn about the committee system by reviewing bills as members of a committee during markup and voting.
- Consider the views of constituents in voting for or against bills.

MATERIALS

- ⌾ **Online Student Edition** and copies of ⌾ **Background Notes 3.8A** and **3.8B,** located at PearsonSuccessNet.com
- *Essential Questions Journal*
- Copies of ⌾ **Activity 3.8A** and **3.8B,** located at PearsonSuccessNet.com
- **Congress 3.a:** Poster of *How a Bill Becomes a Law*
- **Congress: Role Cards** 1–8
- Copies of ⌾ **Assessment 3.8**

BEFORE CLASS

Distribute copies of ⌾ **Background Notes 3.8A** and **3.8B.** For more in-depth information, refer students to the ⌾ **Online Student Edition** Chapter 12, Sections 2, 3, and 4. You may wish to have students read these materials before coming to class. Before class, review students' bills from ⌾ **Activity 3.7B** and assign each to one of the eight committees listed on ⌾ **Background Note 3.8A.**

> **L2 Differentiate** Help students create an outline of ⌾ **Background Note 3.8B** by identifying the main idea and supporting details. Write the outline on the board.

> **L2 Differentiate** Have students listen to the audio summary located at PearsonSuccessNet.com.

TEACH

1. Introduce the Topic Tell students that today they will act as members of a committee in Congress. Refer them to **Congress 3.a** to locate the step that they will be simulating (*Step 2*). Explain that you will act as the Speaker of the House, that you have assigned each of their bills a number, and that committees will "mark up" or review each bill. Remind students to use formal speech and evidence during the debate.

2. Assign District Profiles Tell students that as they review bills in their committees, they will need to consider their constituents in their decision making. Divide students into eight groups and tell them that they will represent the district described on their card. Distribute one district profile to each group (Congress: Role Cards 1–8). Give students two or three minutes to review their district profiles with their group and clarify any questions, then have students count off one through eight and regroup by number. (Each number corresponds to a committee on ⊘ **Background Note 3.8A.**)

3. Assign Committees After students regroup, have them take out ⊘ **Background Note 3.8A** and read about the committee to which their group has been assigned. You may wish to give students time to investigate their committee's actual minority and majority party Web sites at www.house.gov either in class or as homework the previous night.

4. Set Rules and Assign Bills Give each bill a "reading" (read it aloud) and "refer" it to an appropriate committee. The committees have been chosen to increase the likelihood that each committee will be able to consider a similar number of bills. Choose one student in each group to act as the committee chairperson and give the committees a specified amount of time to discuss each bill. Distribute ⊘ **Activity 3.8A,** which gives students directions for the markup session, and ⊘ **Activity 3.8B,** which gives the format for a committee report. You may decide to allow the students to spend the whole class period debating a single bill. The rest of the bills will be considered "pigeonholed" in committee.

5. Have Committees Report on Bills At the end of the assigned time period, ask committees to turn in a committee report on each bill, explaining the action they will take on it. For a shorter class, allow committees to read aloud each bill that they choose to report.

6. Assess Have students complete ⊘ **Assessment 3.8,** which asks them to reflect on the markup process.

EXTEND THE LESSON ▬▬▬▬

L3 Differentiate The lesson can be extended by giving students more time to research the bills they will discuss in committees and by allowing the committees more time to discuss bills.

L4 Differentiate After reading ⊘ **Background Note 3.8B,** have students research and prepare a short presentation about the role of one lobbying group. They should include examples of the group's inside lobbying efforts, outside lobbying efforts, and campaign contributions.

UNIT 3

LESSON 9

Mock Congress

TEACHER INSTRUCTIONS

PURPOSE
To help frame an answer to the ⚡ **Essential Question:** *What makes a successful Congress?*, students will take part in a floor debate on several bills.

LESSON GOALS
- Students will learn about debate in Congress by taking part in a floor debate about several bills written by students.
- Students will consider the needs and wishes of constituents when voting on each bill.

MATERIALS
- ⊘**Online Student Edition,** located at PearsonSuccessNet.com
- **Congress 3.a:** *How a Bill Becomes a Law*
- Copies of ⊘**Activity 3.9A,** *Rules for Debate,* and ⊘**Activity 3.9B,** *Summary of Amendments Proposals* (optional), and ⊘**Activity 3.9C,** *Guidelines for Floor Debate,* located at PearsonSuccessNet.com
- Copies of ⊘**Assessment 3.9,** located at PearsonSuccessNet.com

BEFORE CLASS
Refer students to the ⊘**Online Student Edition** Chapter 12, Sections 3 and 4. You may wish to have students read these materials before coming to class. They should also come to class with notes for the floor debate, including research or a prepared two-minute (or shorter) speech about bills they wrote or bills discussed in their committees. You will also need to prepare a copy of ⊘**Activity 3.9A** and **3.9B** (optional) for each of the bills to be debated in class.

> **L2 Differentiate** Tell students ahead of time which bills will be debated and meet with them to review their notes and presentation for the floor debate.

TEACH

1. Introduce the Topic Refer students to the poster **Congress 3.a** and ask them to identify the steps in the process that they have simulated thus far (*1. Introduction in House and 2. Committee Action*). Tell them that the bills referred by a committee were sent to the Rules Committee, which has issued rules on some of them. To control the amount of time that you spend on the floor debate, you may explain that the majority party wanted to stall some bills, so they were not granted rules. You may also choose whether or not you will allow students to propose amendments to the bills.

2. Assign Rules Distribute ⊘**Activity 3.9A,** ⊘**Activity 3.9B** (if you choose to allow amendments), and ⊘**Activity 3.9C.** Then remind students that the House has a Committee on

Rules that establishes the rules for debate on the floor. Ask them who controls this committee (*the majority party*) and why this committee is important (*It can stop a bill from going to the floor*). Point out the relevant step on **Congress 3.a** and also remind them that their bills would be assigned to a particular calendar and often considered in the House sitting as the Committee of the Whole. Explain that in this simulation, the House will be sitting as the Committee of the Whole. Review the House rules for debate as set out in ⊘**Activity 3.9A** and the guidelines for debate as set out in ⊘**Activity 3.9C.** The rules reflect an official document that the Rules Committee issues for each bill to be debated in the House of Representatives. The guidelines offer instructions for students for the simulation. If there are only a few bills to be debated, you may wish to allow students to add amendments to the bill using ⊘**Activity 3.9B.**

3. *Debate Bills* Remind students that they represent particular districts and should consider those districts in their voting. Then, acting as the Speaker of the House, allow students to debate bills according to the rules and guidelines. At the conclusion of the debate, take a voice vote on each bill. Alternatively, you could make a poster with every student's name in the first column, followed by columns for "yea," "nay," and "present." Students would tape a piece of paper to the board to show their vote on each issue as you do a roll-call vote.

> **L3 Differentiate** You may wish to give students some time to circulate and work to gain ⋅ support for bills by offering to add amendments or vote for other students' bills in exchange for support.

4. *Debrief* Ask students what they thought was most and least effective about the debate and what challenges they would predict for the House, which may debate hundreds or thousands of bills in a session, with some bills running hundreds of pages in length.

5. *Assess* Distribute ⊘**Assessment 3.9,** which asks students to reflect on the activity.

EXTEND THE LESSON

> **L4 Differentiate** Have students research and summarize the views of the Democratic and Republican parties on the issue addressed in the bill chosen for ⊘**Assessment 3.9.** Ask them if they would vote differently on the bill if they were a member of one of the parties.

UNIT 3

LESSON 10

Wrap-Up

TEACHER INSTRUCTIONS

PURPOSE

To help frame an answer to the 🔑 **Essential Question:** *What makes a successful Congress?*, students will reflect on their experiences in the Mock Congress activity.

LESSON GOALS

- Follow the path of a bill that starts in the House as it goes through the Senate then becomes a law.
- Compare the House and the Senate.
- Brainstorm and discuss answers to the 🔑 **Essential Question:** *What makes a successful Congress?*

MATERIALS

- ⦿ **Online Student Edition,** located at PearsonSuccessNet.com
- *Essential Questions Journal*
- Copies of ⦿ **Activity 3.10,** *Comparing the House and the Senate,* located at PearsonSuccessNet.com
- **Congress 3.a:** *How a Bill Becomes a Law*

BEFORE CLASS

Refer students to the ⦿ **Online Student Edition** Chapter 12, Section 4. You may wish to have students read these materials before coming to class. You may also wish to have students complete the *Essential Questions Journal* Chapter 12 Exploration, Parts IV and V, pp. 96–97, before class.

TEACH

1. Review Refer students to **Congress 3.a** and ask what would happen to the bills that were approved in the floor debate. *(A bill that passes successfully through the House will be sent to the Senate.)* Then explain, or ask a student to explain, the rest of the process. *(The bill from the House will be sent to the Senate. If the Senate makes changes to it and then approves it, there will be a conference committee to iron out the differences. If both houses then vote to pass the compromise bill, it will go to the President.)* Tell students that they will look at these steps in closer detail as part of the activity, as the Senate has some procedures that differ from those of the House.

2. Complete the Activity Distribute ⦿ **Activity 3.10,** *Comparing the House and the Senate.* Have students work in pairs to fill in the graphic organizer using the ⦿ **Online Student Edition,** Chapters 10 and 12. Review students' answers to be sure they understand the differences between debate in the House and debate in the Senate, including the filibuster.

3. Brainstorm The question on the activity worksheet asks students to brainstorm answers to the 🔵 **Essential Question:** *What makes a successful Congress?* Ask students to share their ideas with a partner and, in pairs, identify two or three categories of answers. For example, several answers might fit under the headings "personal attributes of members" or "what a successful Congress does." Draw an idea web with the 🔵 **Essential Question** in the middle and the categories as the next level of bubbles.

4. Discuss Extend the idea web, encouraging students to discuss potential answers to the question, using specific examples from the simulation when possible. Take out the poster that you made at the beginning of the unit. Take a new poll and see if students have changed their ideas about what makes a successful Congress. Ask: **Is a successful Congress made up of successful members of Congress?**

> **L3 Differentiate** Divide the class into small groups to make their own idea webs and have a smaller discussion before branching into the class discussion.

> **L2 Differentiate** Write the categories for the idea web on the board in different areas of the classroom, or on posters placed around the classroom. Give students 2 to 3 sticky notes on which to write their ideas and have them place these sticky notes under the correct category headings. Use the ideas on these notes to begin the discussion.

5. Assess Have students answer the 🔵 **Essential Question:** *What makes a successful Congress?*, in their *Essential Questions Journal,* p. 77.

UNIT 4 The Executive Branch

UNIT OVERVIEW

This group of lessons teaches your students about the presidency, including the President's roles, responsibilities, and powers; the roles of the various offices of the executive branch; the function of presidential advisors; government funding; and the making of domestic and foreign policy. The lessons culminate in a classroom Mock White House. At the end of this unit, students will be able to craft an answer to the 🕮 **Essential Question: *What makes a good President?*** You may wish to have students begin their study by completing the ***Essential Questions Journal*** Unit 4 Warmup, p. 103.

UNIT GOALS

- Describe the roles, responsibilities, and powers of the President.
- Understand the structure and responsibilities of the executive branch.
- Know how domestic and foreign policy are created and implemented.
- Understand how the federal government is funded and what its budget-making process is.
- Understand the variety of factors involved in presidential decision making.
- Identify the characteristics and skills necessary to be successful in the office of the President.

TIME ALLOTMENT

This unit of activities is intended to be taught in 10 days (or 5 days on a block schedule).

DAY 1	Lesson 1	Presidential Roles, Responsibilities, and Powers
DAY 2	Lesson 2	The Executive Branch and Presidential Advisors
DAY 3	Lesson 3	Interactive Decision-Making: "You Are the President"
DAY 4	Lesson 4	Creating and Implementing Domestic Policy
DAY 5	Lesson 5	Financing Government
DAY 6	Lesson 6	Creating and Implementing Foreign Policy
DAYS 7–10	Lesson 7	Mock White House

ENDURING UNDERSTANDINGS

- The Constitution defines and delineates the roles, responsibilities, requirements, and powers of the President.
- Since the nation's founding, the power of the President has grown significantly.
- The Executive Office of the President is composed of his or her closest advisors and several support agencies and is the President's right arm in the formation and execution of the nation's public policies.
- The President wields enormous influence in shaping the nation's domestic policy.
- The President and Congress work together to prepare a budget for the nation, but many conflicting needs, viewpoints, and influences make that process contentious and complex.
- The federal government's overarching purpose is the protection of the security and the well-being of the United States of America.

Presidential Roles, Responsibilities, and Powers

TEACHER INSTRUCTIONS

PURPOSE

To frame an answer to the ❦ **Essential Question:** *What makes a good President?,* students need to know the power, roles, and responsibilities integral to the highest office in American government.

LESSON GOALS

- Identify the personal traits and professional qualities that lead to a successful presidency using historical examples.
- Describe the relationship between the presidential roles and powers as defined by the Constitution and provide examples of how they have expanded over time.

MATERIALS

- ⊘**Online Student Edition** and copies of ⊘**Background Notes 4.1A** and **4.1B,** located at PearsonSuccessNet.com
- *Essential Questions Journal*
- *American Government Essential Questions Video* DVD or available ⊘ online at PearsonSuccessNet.com
- Newspapers, magazines, history books, and other reference material with historic or current national and international news and/or images
- Copies of ⊘**Activity 4.1,** *Identifying the Roles of the President,* available at PearsonSuccessNet.com
- Copies of ⊘**Assessment 4.1,** available at PearsonSuccessNet.com

BEFORE CLASS

Distribute copies of ⊘**Background Notes 4.1A** and **4.1B.** For more in-depth information, refer students to the ⊘**Online Student Edition** Chapter 13, Section 1, and Chapter 14, Sections 2–4. You may wish to have students read these materials before coming to class. You may also want students to complete the *Essential Questions Journal* Unit 4 Warmup, p. 103, and Chapter 13 Exploration, pp. 105–106, and Chapter 14 Exploration, pp. 112–116, before class.

> **L2 Differentiate** Instead of students reading the Background Notes on their own, have volunteers take turns reading portions aloud in class. After each portion is read, have a volunteer other than the reader summarize the information.

> **L2 Differentiate** Have students listen to the audio summary available only at PearsonSuccessNet.com.

TEACH

1. Activate Prior Knowledge Tell students that the goal of this unit is to explore the 🌐 **Essential Question:** *What makes a good President?* To help them start thinking about this question, have them take out the ***Essential Questions Journal*** Unit Warmup, p. 103, where they identified the traits that make a successful President, or have them complete it in class. Make a list on the board of the students' top five traits of a good President. Then show the Unit 4 portion of the ***American Government Essential Questions Video,*** which gives a brief overview of several presidencies. Ask which personal traits and professional qualities the Presidents in the video displayed and list them on the board. Do students wish to add or subtract from their list now that they have seen the video? Have them explain their choices.

> **L2 Differentiate ELL** If students are unfamiliar with American Presidents, ask them to name leaders from their own or other countries who exemplify these traits.

2. Introduce the Lesson Tell students that there are many factors to consider when defining what makes a "good President." Understanding how these factors interconnect will not only allow students to evaluate an existing President, but also help them to elect a good President in the future. One of the first things they need to know is the President's roles and responsibilities. Ask students to name the eight roles, and list them on the board.

3. Complete the Activity Have students scan newspapers, magazines, history books, or other reference material to find images that illustrate a President (historic or current) performing as many of the eight presidential roles as possible. Distribute 📄 **Activity 4.1,** *Identifying the Roles of the President,* and have students work in pairs to complete the worksheet.

4. Debrief Have a volunteer from each pair show the images they located and explain which role was being performed. Ask the class if they agree or disagree with the assessments. Create a list on the board of examples of each role, and review the additional roles students think apply to the President. Use these examples to discuss how presidential roles often overlap and are performed simultaneously.

5. Discuss Have students complete the ***Essential Questions Journal*** Chapter 14 Warmup, p. 112. Tell students that the Constitution grants the President specific legislative, executive, judicial, diplomatic, and military powers. Have students categorize each presidential power granted to the President under these headings. Tell students that the power of the President has greatly expanded since 1787. Have them brainstorm reasons for this growth. Then lead a discussion on how much power students think the President should have.

6. Assess Distribute 📄 **Assessment 4.1,** which asks students to determine the two presidential roles that they think are the most important, identify what qualities are required to complete those roles successfully, and determine the roles' associated powers. Have students complete the Chapter 14 Essential Question Essay in their ***Essential Questions Journal,*** p. 118.

EXTEND THE LESSON ━━━━━

> **L4 Differentiate** Have students research one President they consider to be successful. Have them focus on articles, interviews, opinion pieces, and other sources that were written or created at the time of that President's administration. How was the President perceived at the time of his presidency? Did public opinion of that President change over time? Have students present their findings to the class in an oral report or multimedia presentation.

PURPOSE

To frame an answer to the 🕮 **Essential Question:** *What makes a good President?*, students need a basic understanding of the role, organization, and functions of the executive branch, as well as a comprehension of the roles and influence of the President's Cabinet and the White House staff.

LESSON GOALS

- Describe the executive branch and its role in a President's administration.
- Identify key presidential advisors and summarize their basic functions and responsibilities.
- Define bureaucracy and defend their opinion on whether a bureaucracy is essential to good government.

MATERIALS

- 🔟 **Online Student Edition** and copies of 🔟 **Background Notes 4.2A** and **4.2B,** located at PearsonSuccessNet.com
- *Essential Questions Journal*
- Copies of 🔟 **Activity 4.2,** *Understanding the Executive Branch,* available at PearsonSuccessNet.com
- Copies of 🔟 **Assessment 4.2,** available at PearsonSuccessNet.com
- Internet access

BEFORE CLASS

Distribute copies of 🔟 **Background Notes 4.2A** and **4.2B.** For more in-depth information, refer students to the 🔟 **Online Student Edition** Chapter 15, Sections 1–4. You may wish to have students read these materials before coming to class. You may also want students to complete the *Essential Questions Journal* Chapter 15 Warmup and Exploration, pp. 119–125, before class.

> **L2 Differentiate** Have students underline unfamiliar terms used in the Background Notes. List the terms on the board and have volunteers provide a definition for each.

> **L2 Differentiate** Have students listen to the audio summary available only at PearsonSuccessNet.com.

TEACH

1. Introduce the Lesson Explain that in order for the President to successfully perform the roles and responsibilities discussed in the previous lesson, he or she is aided in his or her work by the millions of men and women employed by the executive branch, which is divided into the Executive Office of the President, the executive departments, and the independent agencies. List these on the board. Under each heading, have students write a brief description of the basic roles of this segment of the President's administration. Looking at the listing of specific agencies in the executive branch in the 🔟 **Online Student Edition,** have students discuss which ones they think work most closely with the President.

L2 Differentiate Direct students to look at key words in the title of each department or agency (for example, *economic* in "Council of Economic Advisors") as a clue to the agency or department's function. If they do not know the meaning of a key word, encourage them to look it up in the classroom dictionary.

2. Complete the Activity Distribute ✪Activity 4.2, *Understanding the Executive Branch,* and pair students together to complete the activity. Each pair should use the prompts on the worksheet to help them conduct research on two of the agencies listed. Then each pair should write ten questions or statements for a quiz show. Each should relate to one of the agencies on the worksheet or in the ✪Online Student Edition. Examples include "This is the oldest executive department and advises the President on foreign policy" *(State Department)* or "What type of agency is NASA?" *(independent executive agency).* On slips of paper or index cards, have students write the clue on the front and the answer on the back. Collect the questions and divide the class into four teams. Then play a quiz game with teams competing against each other.

L2 Differentiate ELL To ease the burden of struggling with both content and language, have ELL students write the clues in their native language and then translate into English.

3. Debrief Hold a class discussion on these agencies' role in the President's administration. Write the following on the board: White House Office. Have students create a list of the offices and agencies, such as the Vice President, chief of staff, and press secretary, that come under this umbrella agency. Explain that the White House Office is the most influential unit in the executive branch. It includes the people to whom the President turns on a daily basis. Discuss the roles of these officials. Point out that others in the executive branch also play key roles in various situations, such as the secretary of homeland security in the event of a terrorist threat to the nation. Ask students: **What factors do you think the President considers when appointing people to these posts? How do those appointments reflect on the President?** *(Because these roles have so much influence on public policy, the President must choose people who are highly qualified in each specific area. The performance of these individuals, as well as how the President utilizes them, contributes to the public's perception of whether a President is a "good" or a "bad" President.)*

4. Discuss Have a volunteer define *bureaucracy.* Tell students that the agencies discussed in the lesson are part of the extensive federal bureaucracy, which has grown immensely since the nation's founding. One factor in the growth of presidential power, in fact, is the growth of the bureaucracy. Lead a brief discussion on how this can be the case. Then discuss the ongoing debate regarding the size of the federal bureaucracy and its effect on our daily lives. To enhance this discussion, review the ✪Online Student Edition Issues of Our Time, p. 450.

5. Assess Distribute ✪Assessment 4.2, which asks students to complete a chart detailing the role, functions, and other features of the executive branch. Have students complete the Chapter 15 Essential Question Essay in their *Essential Questions Journal,* p. 127.

EXTEND THE LESSON

L3 Differentiate Direct students as they research the names of the current members of the Cabinet and their qualifications. For each, have students comment on why they think this particular individual was chosen by the President.

L4 Differentiate Have students choose a President and conduct research to find out more about the relationship between that President and his Cabinet. Suggest they consider the following: How much did the President rely on his Cabinet? Was the President more likely to follow the advice of his Cabinet or his own instincts when making major decisions?

TEACHER INSTRUCTIONS

PURPOSE

To help students gain an understanding of the complexity of presidential decision-making, students are given the opportunity to decide how he or she as President will address an energy crisis through an online interactive simulation.

LESSON GOALS

- Identify the various factors and influences that come into play in presidential decisions by directly encountering them through an online simulation.
- Understand how the results of presidential choices affect subsequent decisions.

MATERIALS

- **Online Interactive Decision-Making** simulation, located at PearsonSuccessNet.com
- *Essentials Question Journal*

BEFORE CLASS

Refer students to the **Online Student Edition** Chapter 14, Sections 1–4. You may wish to have students read these materials before coming to class. You may also want students to complete the *Essential Questions Journal* Chapter 14 Warmup and Exploration pp. 112–116, before class.

TEACH

1. Introduce the Lesson Tell students that they are now going to experience firsthand what it is like to be President of the United States. Each student will take on the role as President and determine what decisions he or she will make in order to deal with a national energy crisis. Tell students that as they progress through the simulation, they should note the groups and issues that they found to be influential in their decision-making process.

2. Complete the Activity Have students complete the online activity in class or assign the simulation as homework. NOTE: If you decide to give this as a homework assignment, conduct the Debrief at the beginning of class and then continue with the next day's lesson plan described on the following page.

3. Debrief Lead a discussion about their experience as President. Ask them to identify the groups or issues that influenced their actions most and have them explain why. Then have students identify the decisions they found the most difficult to make.

4. Assess Have students write 3–5 conclusions they can draw about presidential decision-making from the online activity and their study of Unit 4. You may wish to have students share these conclusions in class and follow up with a discussion of how the interactivity helps provide an answer to the ❸ **Essential Question: What makes a good President?**

UNIT 4

LESSON 4

Creating and Implementing Domestic Policy

PURPOSE

To frame an answer to the 🇺🇸 **Essential Question: *What makes a good President?,*** students need to know what domestic policy is and how the federal government influences its formulation and implementation.

LESSON GOALS

- Define domestic policy and explain how it affects American society.
- Identify the tools and methods available to the President to formulate, influence, and implement domestic policy.

MATERIALS

- 🄐 **Online Student Edition** and copies of 🄐 **Background Note 4.4,** located at PearsonSuccessNet.com
- ***Essential Questions Journal***
- Copies of 🄐 **Activity 4.4,** *The President's Role in Domestic Policy,* available at PearsonSuccessNet.com
- Copies of 🄐 **Assessment 4.4,** available at PearsonSuccessNet.com
- Internet access

BEFORE CLASS

Distribute copies of 🄐 **Background Note 4.4,** also available at PearsonSuccessNet.com. For more in-depth information, refer students to the 🄐 **Online Student Edition** Chapter 14, Sections 1, 2, and 4; and Chapter 15, Section 1. You may wish to have students read these materials before coming to class. You may also want students to complete the ***Essential Questions Journal*** Chapter 14 Exploration, pp. 113–116, before class.

> **L2 Differentiate** Ask students to read the Background Note aloud and define the terms in boldface. Then have volunteers explain why these terms are important for understanding the Background Note.

> **L2 Differentiate** Have students listen to the audio summary available only at PearsonSuccessNet.com.

TEACH

1. Introduce the Lesson Explain that domestic policy consists of the decisions, laws, and programs that are directly related to issues within the country. Over the years, domestic policy has reflected the priorities of the American people as well as their expectation that the federal government will provide certain services and programs, such as Social Security and Medicare. Write the following issues on the board: healthcare, the economy, energy/oil, education, climate change, border security/immigration, and civil rights. Have students suggest two ways in which the federal government addresses each issue. Then have students prioritize each issue from highest to lowest according to the importance they think Americans attribute to each.

L4 Differentiate Have students research a domestic policy of their choice, answering the following questions: Is this policy controversial? Which groups support the policy? Which groups oppose it? Where does public opinion stand on this policy? Ask students to summarize the answers to these questions in a brief report.

2. *Complete the Activity* Explain that students will now focus on the President's role in domestic policy by completing ⊘**Activity 4.4,** *The President's Role in Domestic Policy.* Then discuss the various options the President can use to influence domestic policy. Point out that as the nation's leader, the chief executive has enormous influence over the media and can even influence interest groups. Be sure students don't miss the importance of the President's main responsibility, executing the laws, in the creation and implementation of domestic policy. Remind students that presidential influence on domestic policy has grown since the presidency of Franklin D. Roosevelt. Point out that even though the President is responsible for the national constituency, each congressperson is responsible for his or her state constituency, which can lead to conflicts in the creation of domestic policy measures. Ask: **How can a congressperson's responsibility to his or her state have an effect on domestic policy?** *(Sample answer: Promoting the security, economic well-being, and priorities of his or her state are the key responsibilities of each member of Congress. If a state's priorities differ from the President's, that state's representative will make every effort to ensure that a measure will have as little negative effect on the state as possible.)*

> **L2 Differentiate ELL** For students that need help with some of the terms on the worksheet, refer them to the glossary in the ⊘**Online Student Edition.** Suggest that they translate each definition into their native language before answering the Reflection Questions.

> **L4 Differentiate** Have students find excerpts from past State of the Union messages in which the President is exerting influence on domestic policy. Ask students to summarize the President's position as expressed in the speech.

3. *Debrief* On a scale of 1 to 10, have students rate the amount of influence the President has on domestic policy. Then discuss the other groups that also play a part in this area (Congress, the media, interest groups, the federal bureaucracy, etc.). Ask students how the people the President chooses to be part of the administration are critically important in the creation and implementation of domestic policy. Then ask students to think back to Lesson 1. Which of the characteristics of successful Presidents would be most important in the creation and implementation of domestic policy? Ask students to list the top three most important characteristics.

4. *Assess* Distribute ⊘**Assessment 4.4,** which asks students to read excerpts from President Barack Obama's inaugural speech and evaluate it in terms of the creation and implementation of domestic policy.

EXTEND THE LESSON

> **L4 Differentiate** Have students find a political cartoon that comments on a particular President's domestic policy on a specific issue, such as the economy. Provide newspapers, newsmagazines, and Web sites that students can scan for cartoons. When students have located a cartoon, ask them to answer the following: (1) With what aspect of domestic policy is the cartoonist concerned? (2) What position does the cartoonist take on this issue? (3) What American priorities and expectations does the cartoon reflect? (4) According to the cartoonist, what is/was the President's role or position on this policy?

PURPOSE

To frame an answer to the 🏛 **Essential Question: *What makes a good President?*,** students need to consider financial matters, including sources of government funding, the budget-making process, and the role of Congress and the President in developing fiscal policy.

LESSON GOALS

- Define mandatory and discretionary spending and explain how they affect the federal budget.
- Describe the steps involved in the creation of the federal budget from its proposal by the President to the signing of the appropriations legislation.

MATERIALS

- 🔗 **Online Student Edition** and copies of 🔗 **Background Note 4.5,** located at PearsonSuccessNet.com
- *Essential Questions Journal*
- Copies of 🔗 **Activity 4.5,** *Understanding the Federal Budget Process,* Parts I–III, available at PearsonSuccessNet.com
- Copies of 🔗 **Assessment 4.5,** available at PearsonSuccessNet.com

BEFORE CLASS

Distribute copies of 🔗 **Background Note 4.5,** also available at PearsonSuccessNet.com. For more in-depth information, refer students to the 🔗 **Online Student Edition** Chapter 16, Sections 1–4. You may wish to have students read these materials before coming to class. You may also want students to complete the *Essential Questions Journal* Chapter 16 Warmup and Exploration, pp. 128–133, before class.

> **L2 Differentiate** Help students create an outline of the Background Note by identifying the main idea and supporting details. Write the outline on the board.

> **L2 Differentiate** Have students listen to the audio summary available only at PearsonSuccessNet.com.

TEACH

1. Introduce the Lesson Remind students that the federal government operates under a budget, much as their own families probably do. Explain that, in a similar way, some of the government's expenses are controllable and others are uncontrollable. Provide the following example: If your parents pay a mortgage on their house, the amount of that payment is set by the bank and must be paid every month. Your parents have no control over that payment, and so it is considered uncontrollable (or mandatory) spending. The amounts spent on other items, such as clothing, Internet access, and entertainment, are controllable (or discretionary), since your parents can decide how much to spend on these items. The federal government also has controllable spending,

UNIT 4
LESSON
5

Financing Government

such as the amount spent on national defense, and uncontrollable spending, such as the amount spent on Social Security. Tell students that uncontrollable spending amounts to more than 60 percent of all government spending.

> **L2 Differentiate ELL** Provide ELL students with synonyms for *controllable, uncontrollable, discretionary,* and *mandatory* to help them better comprehend these terms. *Controllable—* manageable; *uncontrollable—*uncontainable; *mandatory—*required, essential; *discretionary—*voluntary, optional.

2. Complete the Activity Explain that students will now consider various aspects of the budget process as they complete Parts I–III of ✪ **Activity 4.5,** *Understanding the Federal Budget Process.* After students have completed the worksheet, review the actual steps involved in the creation of the federal budget, and discuss the difficulty of crafting a budget, given the conflicting needs and many agendas of the President and members of Congress.

> **L2 Differentiate** Be sure students understand each of the spending programs suggested in Part I by asking them to identify which federal department or agency would supervise each program on the list. Have students work in pairs and allow them to use their textbook and other sources to help locate the proper government entity.

> **L4 Differentiate** Have students research the most recent budget proposed by the President and reactions to it. Ask students to determine whether other countries are concerned with the United States budget. If so, with which categories of spending are they concerned? What event(s) triggered this interest? Have students write a brief response to these questions.

3. Debrief Examine the tensions in the budget process between the President and Congress. Discuss how this dynamic might change if the President and a majority of the members of Congress are from the same political party versus having a divided government. Consider the difficulty presented by the rising costs of uncontrollable spending, including interest on the public debt. What avenues are available to the President and Congress to address these issues?

4. Assess Distribute ✪ **Assessment 4.5,** which provides several thought-provoking questions on the creation of the federal budget. Discuss each as a class before students write their answers. Have students complete the Chapter 16 Essential Question Essay in their ***Essential Questions Journal,*** p. 135.

EXTEND THE LESSON ▬▬▬▬▬▬▬▬▬▬▬▬▬▬▬▬▬▬▬▬

> **L3 Differentiate** Have students work in small groups to design a Web page that explains various aspects of the budget process. The Web page should be offered as a public service and should cover the following topics: the federal budget process, federal government spending and income, and why the budget is so important. Students should divide up the tasks involved in designing the site as follows: copywriter(s), designers(s), researcher(s). The researchers will do their portion of the project first, followed by the copywriters, and then the designers. Post students' final sketches of their pages with the real content around the classroom.

> **L4 Differentiate** Have students actually create their Web page as part of the school district Web site (obtain permission from the proper channels beforehand). If possible, have them present their idea to school administration officials as part of the project.

UNIT 4

LESSON

6

Creating and Implementing Foreign Policy

PURPOSE

To frame an answer to the 🏛 **Essential Question:** *What makes a good President?,* students need to understand the vital importance of foreign policy, and how the President and the executive branch work together to shape it.

LESSON GOALS

- Identify and summarize key foreign policies of the United States.
- Identify the goals of American foreign policy and describe the tools available to the President and other key officials to implement those goals.

MATERIALS

- ⊘**Online Student Edition** and copies of ⊘**Background Notes 4.6A** and **4.6B,** located at PearsonSuccessNet.com
- *Essential Questions Journal*
- Copies of ⊘**Activity 4.6,** *Foreign Policy Part I: Goals* and *Foreign Policy Part II: Tools,* available at PearsonSuccessNet.com
- Copies of ⊘**Assessment 4.6,** available at PearsonSuccessNet.com

BEFORE CLASS

Distribute copies of ⊘**Background Notes 4.6A** and **4.6B,** also available at PearsonSuccessNet. com. For more in-depth information, refer students to the ⊘**Online Student Edition** Chapter 14, Section 3, and Chapter 17, Sections 1–4. You may wish to have students read these materials before coming to class. You may also want students to complete the *Essential Questions Journal* Chapter 17 Warmup and Exploration, pp. 136–141, before class.

> **L2 Differentiate** Ask students to read the Background Notes aloud and define the terms in boldface. Then have volunteers explain why these terms are important for understanding the Background Notes.

> **L2 Differentiate** Have students listen to the audio summary available only at PearsonSuccessNet.com.

TEACH

1. Introduce the Lesson Write the definition for *foreign policy* on the board: the stands and actions that a nation takes in its relationships with other countries. Beside that definition, write *People.* Discuss recent events in the news in foreign policy, using an Internet news site or a recent national newspaper. Try to elicit from students the names and positions of some of the key players, eventually listing the secretary of state, the secretary of defense, the President, the joint chiefs of staff, the secretary of homeland security, and the director of national intelligence. Ask: **Is American foreign policy based on an isolationist or internationalist viewpoint?** To help students decipher these terms, break out the words *isolate* and *international* and have students define them.

L2 Differentiate Help students grasp the concept of foreign policy through concrete examples. Explain that declaring war, deciding whether to aid a nation that has been struck by natural disaster, limiting the number of nuclear warheads in a nation's arsenal, and visits between the President and the head of state of another country are all examples of foreign policy in action. Ask students to offer additional examples.

2. Complete the Activity Explain that students will now focus on the key goals and tools of American foreign policy by completing ⊘ **Activity 4.6,** *Foreign Policy Part I: Goals.* As students complete Part I, distribute ⊘ **Activity 4.6,** *Foreign Policy Part II: Tools,* and have each pair work together to determine how this new information may affect the actions of the United States. After students have completed the worksheets, discuss factors and issues that influence foreign policy, focusing in particular on world events, the global economy, and U.S. foreign policy goals. Ask students how they think global interdependency has affected American foreign policy. Then lead a discussion on how America's role as a superpower has led to a growth in presidential power.

L4 Differentiate Ask students to find a recent newspaper or magazine article that deals with some aspect of foreign policy. Have them identify the foreign policy goal associated with the issue and the tools the President or other executive branch official utilized in coping with the issue.

3. Debrief Discuss the goals of American foreign policy and the various tools that the executive branch has at its disposal in the conduct of foreign policy. Ask students to consider the role of Congress in foreign policy. Which executive branch actions require congressional approval or involvement? Be sure students understand that international organizations, such as the UN and NATO, work to deter aggression and to meet it collectively should the need arise. Can students see drawbacks and benefits to belonging to such organizations? Discuss their impressions.

4. Assess Distribute ⊘ **Assessment 4.6,** which asks students to find examples of news articles that reflect American foreign policy goals. Discuss students' discoveries and understanding of what constitutes foreign policy. Have students complete the Chapter 17 Essential Question Essay in their *Essential Questions Journal,* p. 143. Then have students complete the Unit 4 Essential Question Essay Warmup, pp. 144–145, then answer the ⬤ **Essential Question:** *What makes a good President?* in their *Essential Questions Journal,* p. 146.

EXTEND THE LESSON ━━━━━━━━━━━

L3 Differentiate Have students write a presidential statement of foreign policy on a current international political event. For help in selecting an issue, suggest that they look through national or international newspapers or newsmagazines. In their statements, students should describe the event, whether the United States approves or disapproves of the actions, how it affects current American foreign policy in the region, and what the President proposes will be the American response to the event.

L4 Differentiate Remind students of the ⬤ **Essential Question:** *What makes a good President?* Ask them to write a response to this question that relates solely to foreign policy—i.e., how does a good President influence the outcome of American foreign policy? Suggest that they consider the key goals of American foreign policy and the factors and issues that play a part in the formulation of that policy.

PURPOSE

To help frame an answer to the ✪ **Essential Question:** *What makes a good President?,* students will conduct a **Mock White House** simulation in which they must apply the information learned throughout this unit to decide whether the United States will provide additional emergency funds to Indonesia following a devastating tsunami.

LESSON GOALS

- Apply knowledge about presidential roles, responsibilities, and powers; the executive branch; the formation of domestic and foreign policy; and government finances to a role-playing activity in which the President and members of the executive branch must make a decision about how the United States should respond to a foreign crisis.

- Learn about the complex interplay of factors involved in presidential decision making.

- Evaluate and synthesize information, form conclusions, and demonstrate reasoned judgment.

MATERIALS

- ✪**Online Student Edition**
- *Role Cards* Tent cards for the President, Vice President, secretary of state, chief of staff, national security advisor, and press secretary, with snapshot descriptions
- **White House 4.a:** *Satellite Images of Indonesia* Before and after photographs showing the destruction caused by the fictional tsunami that occurred on the western coast of Indonesia.
- **White House 4.b:** *Destruction Close-Up* Photograph that zooms in on the tsunami aftermath.
- **White House 4.c:** *Southeast Asia: Political Map* Map offering a frame of reference for viewing the other sources. Map shows political boundaries in Southeast Asia as well as the earthquake epicenter that triggered the fictional tsunami. Students will use this map to assist in their decision making.
- **White House 4.d:** *Newspaper Article* News article from an international newspaper discussing the human element of the event as well as how the aid is being used in the region.
- ✪**White House 4.e:** *Daily Briefing,* located at PearsonSuccessNet.com
- ✪**White House 4.f:** *Fact Sheet on Indonesia,* located at PearsonSuccessNet.com
- ✪**White House 4.g:** *Roles and Responsibilities,* located at PearsonSuccessNet.com
- ✪**White House 4.h:** *Decision Matrix,* located at PearsonSuccessNet.com
- ✪**White House 4.i:** *Campaign Manager Memorandum,* located at PearsonSuccessNet.com
- ✪**White House 4.j:** *Summary Report on Indonesia,* located at PearsonSuccessNet.com
- ✪**White House 4.k:** *Letter from the Speaker of the House,* located at PearsonSuccessNet.com
- ✪**White House 4.l:** *Newspaper Article,* located at PearsonSuccessNet.com

- **White House 4.m**: *Letter from Malaysian Ambassador to the United States,* located at PearsonSuccessNet.com
- **White House 4.n**: *Telex from the Red Cross,* located at PearsonSuccessNet.com

BEFORE CLASS

Assign each student the role of President, Vice President, secretary of state, chief of staff, national security advisor, or press secretary. Distribute **White House 4.e:** *Daily Briefing,* which explains the situation in Southeast Asia; **White House 4.f:** *Fact Sheet,* which lays out some basic information about the region affected; and **White House 4.g:** *Role Responsibilities,* which explains the job responsibilities for each role. You may wish to have students review these handouts before class.

TEACH

1. Introduce the Lesson Distribute the **Group Activity Rubric,** and preview with students so that they know what is expected of them throughout the **Mock White House.** Explain that this activity will give them insight and understanding into the interplay of forces that occurs each time the President must make an important decision. Discuss **White House 4.e:** *Daily Briefing* to answer students' questions about the scenario. Focus their attention on the discussion questions on the handout and hold a class discussion about them.

> **L2 Differentiate ELL** Suggest that students circle any words in the daily briefing and fact sheet that they do not understand. After they have looked the words up in a dictionary, have them reread the handouts with their definitions close at hand.

> **L4 Differentiate** Have students research the December 2004 earthquake and subsequent tsunami in Indonesia, finding out as much as they can about the amount and type of aid sent by the United States, the death toll, the strength of the earthquake, and the extent the region has been able to rebuild. Students can compile their information into an essay or a multimedia report to share with the rest of the class.

DAY 1

1. Display the Map Post the map of Southeast Asia **(White House 4.c)** and show students where the tsunami struck. Point out the location of the earthquake that triggered the tsunami and the large area affected by the disaster.

2. Divide Students Into Groups Break the class into six groups, as follows:

- Group 1: Presidents
- Group 2: Vice Presidents
- Group 3: Secretaries of State
- Group 4: Chiefs of Staff
- Group 5: Nation Security Advisors
- Group 6: Press Secretaries

> **L2 Differentiate** You may differentiate this step by assigning students to teams based on their interests or ability levels. The press secretary's job is difficult due to the job requirements: ability to present and defend a position. Hand out the appropriate role card to each group. Consider photocopying the cards so that each group member can have a copy.

3. Distribute Hand out **Role Cards** and **White House 4.g:** *Role Responsibilities* to the appropriate group. Based on the descriptions on the handout and on the back of the Role Cards, have each group read and discuss their particular role and what is expected of them in that role. Refer them to the online or print textbook and other print or Internet sources to review what each person's job entails. For instance, the President has multiple roles. How will the necessity of juggling these roles affect any decision that has to be made?

4. Post Documents Post **White House 4.a,** which shows before and after photos of tsunami; **White House 4.b,** a close-up of the destruction caused by the tsunami; and **White House 4.d,** which is a news article discussing the Indonesian struggle to rebuild. *Note: You may wish to have students circulate those items within each of the groups.* Ask: What do these photographs illustrate? What degree of damage is shown? Which is more compelling, the photographs or the written description of the tsunami's effect? Why? Based on what they know thus far, have students discuss in their groups what steps they think they need to take in their specific roles. For homework, you may wish to have students write a memo stating their group's preliminary point of view and suggestion for action.

DAY 2

1. Assemble Role Groups Have students convene with their groups from Day 1. Then distribute the following handouts to the groups listed.

> **White House 4.i:** *Campaign Manager Memorandum* to VICE PRESIDENT group
>
> **White House 4.j:** *Summary Report on Indonesia* to NATIONAL SECURITY ADVISOR group
>
> **White House 4.k:** *Letter from Congress* to PRESIDENT group
>
> **White House 4.l:** *Newspaper Article* to PRESS SECRETARY group
>
> **White House 4.m:** *Letter from Malaysian Ambassador to the United States* to SECRETARY OF STATE group
>
> **White House 4.n:** *Telex from the Red Cross* to CHIEF OF STAFF group

Allow groups time to read and discuss the new information presented in their handout. Does the information change the group's position regarding aid to Indonesia? Not everyone in the group needs to agree, but each student in the group should decide on his or her position.

2. Create New Groups Using the jigsaw strategy, reconfigure the groups into six new groups comprised of one representative of each role (i.e., Group 1 now has a President, Vice President, secretary of state, and so on).

3. Distribute Hand out **White House 4.h:** *Decision Matrix.* Students should work in their new groups to begin weighing the various options. Have the groups identify each "issue to consider" as a pro or con based on their role. They should also share the unique information that they received in their role groups (i.e., the student handouts from the campaign manager, Congress, Red Cross, etc.).

4. Discuss Have students continue to discuss their options and the possible repercussions of those actions. To help students focus their discussion, provide the following categories and explain that they should consider how their decision might affect each of the following:

- the President's chance for reelection
- the people of Indonesia
- the people of the United States

- national security
- the U.S. economy
- the federal budget

By the end of the class period, each group should have settled on their position regarding aid to Indonesia. Have students finalize their decision and work to create a press statement that the press secretary will read in tomorrow's class. Tell students that they will conduct a press briefing tomorrow in front of the class. At this briefing, the press secretary will read the press release, and then the floor will be open to the reporters (the class) for questions to any of the members of the group. For homework, you may wish to have the press secretary write the group's official statement and have the other individual group members anticipate questions and create a brief statement in case their input is required during the press briefing. Make sure they keep in mind their roles' responsibilities and concerns when writing their statements.

DAY 3

1. Press Briefings Students will sit with their group in front of the class. The press secretary will present the group's recommendation to the rest of the class in the form of a press briefing. After informing the press of the President's decision and the reasons for it, the press secretary should take questions. Should the press secretary need help, any other member of his or her group may address a question. When students are listening to one of the other groups, they are reporters. As each group addresses the reporters, the rest of the students should record the strengths and weaknesses of each argument and decision. To ensure that all members of the group take part in this presentation and to get the reporters warmed up, use some of the following prompts, adjusting them according to the group's decision:

"Mr./Ms. Press Secretary, could you clarify what you mean by . . ."

"Mr./Ms. President, in your current campaign, you have supported the policy of reducing foreign involvement. Does this foreign aid package indicate a change in that stance?"

"Mr./Ms. Secretary, do you think this amount of aid, which is significantly reduced from what was requested, will have an effect on the international image of the United States?"

"Mr./Ms. \<last name>, considering the recent attacks on the Red Cross and other volunteers, do you think there is any danger in sending Americans/the military to Indonesia?"

"Mr./Ms. Vice President, will any federal programs need to be reduced or canceled to allow for the cost of this package to Indonesia?"

2. Discuss As a class, discuss the strengths and weaknesses in the decisions that students noted. Did most groups make the same final decision about aid to Indonesia? If so, were their reasons similar? If not, why not? Ask students to consider whether their groups' decision advanced the foreign policy goals of the United States as discussed in Lesson 6, such as protecting national security, advancing economic stability, protecting human rights, ensuring collective security. Ask: Which American foreign policy goals were achieved by your group's decision? Were they advanced fully, partially, or not at all. Do you think your decision is likely to be good for the American people? Why or why not? Then, lead a discussion on the factors and forces that proved to be the most influential in each group's decision-making process. Finally, ask a representative from each group to evaluate how well their group's decision would reflect on their administration and President. *Note: If more time is required to have each group make their presentation, have the remaining groups present on Day 4 and hold this discussion following the last presentation.*

DAY 4

1. Debrief Write the following categories on the board: *Congress, public opinion, the UN, the media, special interest groups, the budget, upcoming elections,* and *other countries.* Ask students to write a short paragraph explaining how each of these forces influences a President's decisions. Have students share their paragraphs and discuss each category as a class. Can students think of other forces that influence a President's decisions?

2. Assess Have students answer the **Essential Question: What makes a good President?** in their *Essential Questions Journal.* You may also use one of the following formats:

>   **Assessment option 1:** Present answer in an essay.
>
>   **Assessment option 2:** Present answer in a multimedia format.
>
>   **Assessment option 3:** Present answer in a visual format.
>
>   **Assessment option 4:** Create a skit that shows the qualities of a "good" President.

3. Conclude Point out that, through this **Mock White House,** students should have gained a better understanding of the issues with which a President must contend when making any major decision. Explain that, to be fair, any assessment of the quality of presidential leadership should be separated from partisan politics. Instead, the rating should be based on broader ideals, such as the standard offered by Ronald Reagan some 30 years ago: Are you (and is the United States) better off than you were four years ago (or before the President took office)?

EXTEND THE LESSON

L3 Differentiate Have students identify a current issue in the news for which the President must choose a course of action. Ask students to find out what forces are at play and to evaluate the various options available to the President. Based on their opinions about what makes a good President, have students decide how the President should act. Suggest that they follow the issue to its resolution to see if the President's decision corresponds to their "recommendation."

L2 Differentiate Choose a current issue in the news for students to consider. Help them make a graphic organizer that shows the important aspects of this issue and the options available to the President.

L4 Differentiate Have students choose a historical issue that has confronted a past President. After identifying the various choices available to the President at the time, students should choose an option other than what the President actually chose and try to predict what would have happened if the President had chosen this alternative. Students may present their work in an infographic format, titled "What If?" or something equally appropriate. Post their work around the classroom.

UNIT 5

The Judicial Branch

UNIT OVERVIEW

This group of lessons is intended to teach your students how the judicial system works. Students will identify what judges do, various types of law, what constitutes a federal case, where federal cases are tried, how and why cases are appealed, what types of cases are heard by the Supreme Court, First Amendment freedoms, and rights of the accused. An online activity gives students an interactive look into the history of the struggle for civil rights. The lessons culminate in a mock trial. At the end of this unit, students will be able to craft an answer to the ✪ **Essential Question: *What should be the role of the judicial branch?*** You may wish to have students begin their study by completing the *Essential Questions Journal* Unit 5 Warmup, p. 148.

UNIT GOALS

- Appreciate the role of the courts in a democracy.
- Learn how the federal judicial system works.
- Learn the First Amendment freedoms and civil rights, and how due process safeguards the rights of the accused.
- Understand the proceedings in court cases.

TIME ALLOTMENT

This unit of activities is intended to be taught in 10 days (or 5 days on a block schedule).

DAY 1	Lesson 1	The Role of Courts
DAY 2	Lesson 2	Federal Court Structure
DAY 3	Lesson 3	How Judges Decide
DAYS 4–5	Lesson 4	First Amendment Freedoms
DAY 6	Lesson 5	Interactive Decision Making: Civil Rights
DAY 7	Lesson 6	Rights of the Accused
DAYS 8–10	Lesson 7	Mock Trial

ENDURING UNDERSTANDINGS

- Civil and criminal laws are put in place to provide order, protect society, and settle conflicts. Law officers have the duty to enforce the laws, and courts have the duty to interpret the law and to decide punishment for those found guilty of breaking laws.

- The inferior constitutional courts form the core of the federal judicial system, hearing nearly all of the cases tried in federal courts. The Supreme Court, however, is the final authority.

- The guarantees in the Bill of Rights reflect the nation's commitment to personal freedom and to the principle of limited government. Due process requires that government must act fairly and in accordance with established rules.

- When the use of police power conflicts with civil rights protections, courts must balance society's needs with individual freedoms.

The Role of Courts

TEACHER INSTRUCTIONS

PURPOSE

To frame an answer to the ⓠ **Essential Question:** *What should be the role of the judicial branch?*, students need to know the responsibilities of judges and courts in deciding cases involving the various types of law in this country.

LESSON GOALS

- Understand the responsibilities of courts and judges in a democracy through class discussion.
- Identify types of law and cases heard by courts in the United States by scanning newspapers for examples.
- Give a general overview of court systems in the United States.

MATERIALS

- ⓞ**Online Student Edition** and copies of ⓞ**Background Notes 5.1A** and **5.1B,** located at PearsonSuccessNet.com
- *Essential Questions Journal*
- *American Government Essential Questions Video* DVD or ⓞonline at PearsonSuccessNet.com
- Newspapers with national, international, and local news that include court cases, or Web sites of a few newspapers; each pair of students should have several sections
- Copies of ⓞ**Activity 5.1,** *Analyzing Cases and Courts,* located at PearsonSuccessNet.com
- Copies of ⓞ**Assessment 5.1,** located at PearsonSuccessNet.com

BEFORE CLASS

Distribute copies of ⓞ**Background Notes 5.1A** and **5.1B.** For more in-depth information, refer students to the ⓞ**Online Student Edition** Chapter 18, Section 1, and Chapter 24, Sections 4 and 5. You may wish to have students read these materials before coming to class. You may also want students to complete the *Essential Questions Journal* Chapter 18 Warmup, p. 149, before class.

> **L2 Differentiate** Help students create an outline of the Background Notes by identifying the main ideas and supporting details. Write the outlines on the board.

> **L2 Differentiate** Have students listen to the audio summary available at PearsonSuccessNet.com.

TEACH

1. Activate Prior Knowledge Tell students that the goal of this unit is to explore the ⓠ **Essential Question:** *What should be the role of the judicial branch?* To help them start thinking about this question, review the homework they completed in the *Essential Questions Journal* Unit 5 Warmup, p. 148, where they considered the various roles of courts and judges. On the board, tabulate the answers that students selected.

2. Introduce the Lesson Read aloud the following scenario to students: You approach a red light while driving. To avoid waiting behind other cars that are turning left, you drive onto the shoulder and turn right. A police car flashes its lights, and the officer writes out a ticket for driving on the shoulder—a moving violation. You explain, "I didn't know that was illegal." Will the officer still ticket you? Why or why not? Discuss why ignorance of the law is not acceptable.

Change the scenario slightly: As you turn onto the shoulder, you unknowingly hit a bicyclist coming up behind you, and you drive on. You're charged with reckless driving and with fleeing the scene of an accident that resulted in bodily harm. What types of crimes are these? *(Reckless driving is a misdemeanor; fleeing is a felony.)* If you plead not guilty, what will happen? *(You are entitled to a trial in a court of law.)*

3. Discuss Background Notes Have students scan 🍭 Background Notes 5.1A and 5.1B as they consider the role of courts and laws in the United States. Ask: **What are some basic principles of the American judicial system? On what basis do courts and judges decide cases? What types of law do we have? What is the dual system of courts? What are the levels of courts in the American judiciary?**

4. Complete Activity Sheet 5.1 Explain that students will now spend 5–10 minutes scanning newspapers to find articles about real cases and courts. Alternatively, students could look at newspapers online or at a local print newspaper at home the night before for homework. Organize students into pairs. Distribute 🍭 Activity 5.1, *Analyzing Cases and Courts*, and several newspaper sections to each pair. Have students follow the directions given on 🍭 Activity 5.1. Circulate to answer questions and to help keep students on track. When pairs have completed the activity, ask a spokesperson from each pair to describe the case aloud. Have the class vote on whether the cases are criminal, civil, constitutional, or regulatory. In addition, have the class decide which court will hear the case.

> **L2 Differentiate LPR** Pair a less-proficient reader with a more skilled reader during the newspaper scanning.

5. Present Video Show students the *American Government Essential Questions Video,* which highlights Supreme Court decisions that changed American history and shows why courts matter.

6. Debrief Ask students to explain why we need a court system. As a prompt, you may wish to use Alexander Hamilton's statement that we need courts and judges to handle "the variety of controversies which grow out of the folly and wickedness of mankind." Ask: **What would society be like without a way to address injustices?**

7. Assess Distribute 🍭 Assessment 5.1, which requires students to classify various legal actions according to type of law and to identify which type of court would hear the case.

EXTEND THE LESSON ▬▬▬▬▬▬▬▬▬▬▬▬▬▬▬▬▬▬

> **L3 Differentiate** Have students rank the offenses listed on 🍭 Activity 5.1 from the most serious to the least serious offenses based on their opinion, not according to how the law has classified the offenses. Then ask them to justify their rankings.

UNIT 5

LESSON 2

TEACHER INSTRUCTIONS

PURPOSE

To frame an answer to the ✦ **Essential Question:** *What should be the role of the judicial branch?*, students need to know what constitutes a federal case, where federal cases are tried, the path of federal appeals, and what types of cases are heard by the Supreme Court.

LESSON GOALS

- Identify whether federal courts, state courts, or either court have jurisdiction over certain cases by filling in a Venn diagram.
- Explain the jurisdiction of the federal inferior courts and the Supreme Court through discussion.
- Understand federal court structure by labeling a diagram with the inferior courts.

MATERIALS

- ⦿ **Online Student Edition** and copies of ⦿ **Background Note 5.2,** located at PearsonSuccessNet.com
- *Essential Questions Journal*
- Copies of ⦿ **Activity 5.2A,** *State and Federal Jurisdiction,* located at PearsonSuccessNet.com
- Copies of ⦿ **Activity 5.2B,** *Federal Jurisdiction and Appeals,* located at PearsonSuccessNet.com
- Copies of ⦿ **Assessment 5.2,** located at PearsonSuccessNet.com

BEFORE CLASS

Distribute copies of ⦿ **Background Note 5.2.** For more in-depth information, refer students to the ⦿ **Online Student Edition** Chapter 18, Sections 2, 3, and 4. You may wish to have students read these materials before coming to class. You may also want students to complete the *Essential Questions Journal* Chapter 18 Exploration, pp. 150–154, before class.

> **L2 Differentiate** Instead of students reading the Background Note on their own, have volunteers take turns reading portions aloud in class. After each portion is read, have a volunteer other than the reader summarize the information.

> **L2 Differentiate** Have students listen to the audio summary available at PearsonSuccessNet.com.

TEACH

1. Introduce the Lesson Have students reconsider the scenario you presented in the introduction of **Lesson 5.1** but with this twist: The student is riding a bicycle in a lane designated for cyclists. A vehicle swerves into the cyclists' lane and seriously harms the student. The driver is charged with reckless driving, but the student must spend several months in a hospital. In so doing, the student forgoes all the wages lost at his or her part-time job, as well as a scholarship to college that was pending. What can the student do to regain the lost wages and scholarship funds? *(He or she can file a civil suit.)* Suppose the student's case is heard, but lost. What recourse does the student have? *(The case can be appealed.)*

2. Review State versus Federal Jurisdiction Remind students that they looked at a general overview of court structure in the previous lesson. In this lesson they will take a closer look at courts and their jurisdictions. Have students work in pairs to complete the Venn diagram on ✪ Activity 5.2A, *State and Federal Jurisdiction,* and then answer the Reflection Question. After the activity is finished, discuss why each dispute or case was under its particular jurisdiction.

> **L2 ELL Differentiate** Pair ELL students with students who can help define difficult words on the activity.

3. Federal Court Jurisdiction and Paths of Appeal Tell students that now they are going to focus exclusively on jurisdiction of specific federal courts. Have them scan ✪ Background Note 5.2 as they consider these questions: Over what subject matter and parties do federal courts have jurisdiction? Which courts are under the Supreme Court? Why are there so many types of federal courts? Distribute ✪ Activity 5.2B, *Federal Jurisdiction and Appeals,* and have students complete the chart and paths of appeals.

> **L4 Differentiate** For homework, ask students to research current federal cases in the news and determine which court would hear the cases, and why.

4. Debrief Draw a pyramid on the board with the title "Federal Court Structure." Label the top of the pyramid "Supreme Court" and have students complete the rest of the pyramid with the inferior courts. Then, if they have not already done so, have students complete the Chapter 18 Exploration in their *Essential Questions Journal,* pp. 150–154.

5. Assess Distribute ✪ Assessment 5.2, which asks students to create a quiz describing five scenerios in which Joe or Jane Smith breaks a federal law. Have students exchange and complete one anothers' quizzes by naming the jurisdiction of each case and explaining why.

EXTEND THE LESSON ▬▬▬▬▬▬▬▬▬▬

> **L3 Differentiate** For students to understand how an actual case is presented before the Supreme Court, copy and distribute Chapter 18, Section 3, Core Worksheet A (Unit 5 All-in-One, p. 17), which includes excerpts adapted from the oral arguments in the 1989 Supreme Court case *Ward* v. *Rock Against Racism* (RAR). Have students read the script aloud, taking turns playing the parts of the justices and attorneys.

TEACHER INSTRUCTIONS

PURPOSE

To frame an answer to the ⚉ **Essential Question:** *What should be the role of the judicial branch?*, students need to know the factors judges weigh in making decisions.

LESSON GOALS

- Explain the power of judicial review.
- Analyze how judges make decisions through class discussion.
- Understand the philosophies of judicial restraint and judicial activism by classifying Supreme Court decisions.
- Simulate Supreme Court deliberations.

MATERIALS

- ⊘ **Online Student Edition** and copies of ⊘ **Background Note 5.3,** located at PearsonSuccessNet.com
- ***Essential Questions Journal***
- Copies of ⊘ **Activity 5.3,** *Supreme Court Deliberations,* located at PearsonSuccessNet.com
- Copies of ⊘ **Assessment 5.3,** located at PearsonSuccessNet.com

BEFORE CLASS

Distribute copies of ⊘ **Background Note 5.3.** For more in-depth information, refer students to the ⊘ **Online Student Edition** Chapter 18, Section 3.

> **L2 Differentiate** Ask students to underline the main idea of each paragraph in the Background Note. Have volunteers read aloud and explain their choices.

> **L2 Differentiate** Have students listen to the audio summary available at PearsonSuccessNet.com.

TEACH

1. Introduce the Lesson Ask students what factors they consider when making an important decision, such as which college to attend. They might cite such issues as cost, distance from home, degrees offered, parental influence, where their friends are attending, and so on. Tell students that in this lesson, they will learn what factors judges weigh when they make important judicial decisions.

2. Discuss the Supreme Court Have students read ⊘ **Background Note 5.3** and consider these questions: Why is interpreting the U.S. Constitution so difficult? Why does the power of judicial review give the judicial branch strength equal to the legislative and executive branches? With which judicial philosophy do you most agree? Why?

L2 Differentiate Write these questions on the board so students can read them and/or copy them into their notebooks once you have read them aloud.

3. *Distinguish Judicial Activism and Restraint* Ask students: **What types of Supreme Court decisions, in general, would show judicial restraint?** *(Possible answers: upholding a state law or a lower court's decision; following precedent; refusing to rule on a case, claiming it is the jurisdiction of the state or another branch of government)* **What decisions of the Court, in general, would show judicial activism?** *(Possible answers: changing a previous Supreme Court ruling; overturning a lower court's decision; halting or requiring legislative, executive, and/or state action)*

L2 ELL Differentiate Have students provide synonyms for the terms *restraint* (limit, restrict, curb, self-control) and *activism* (change, innovate, create, revise).

4. *Classify Court Decisions* Have students classify the following decisions as judicial restraint or judicial activism.

- The Court upholds laws requiring racially segregated facilities, *Plessy* v. *Ferguson*, 1896. *(restraint)*
- The Court declares that freedom of speech and press cannot be denied by either the national government or state governments, *Gitlow* v. *New York*, 1925. *(activism)*
- The Court declares constitutional a California law that makes it illegal to advocate criminal acts, *Whitney* v. *California*, 1927. *(restraint)*
- The Court rules that people who are too poor to hire a lawyer cannot be assured a fair trial unless counsel is provided for them, *Gideon* v. *Wainwright*, 1963. *(activism)*

5. *Group Deliberations* Organize students into odd-numbered groups to complete ✪ **Activity 5.3,** *Supreme Court Deliberations,* in which students discuss and formulate opinions on controversial issues that have come before the Supreme Court. Each group must come to a majority opinion on each issue. Circulate and facilitate the discussions to keep students on task. After the issues are discussed, tabulate the statements and majority opinions on the board.

L2 Differentiate Have students work individually and select one issue in ✪ **Activity 5.3** that interests them. Give students time to analyze and make notes about their opinions on the issue. Then discuss the issues as a class.

L4 Differentiate Ask student pairs to take opposing sides on one of the issues in ✪ **Activity 5.3.** Students should research the issue, and then debate it in front of the class. Have the class discuss how the evidence presented in the debate influenced their opinions.

6. *Assess* Distribute ✪ **Assessment 5.3,** in which students prepare an opening statement for a confirmation hearing for a federal judge. Suggest that students have been nominated by the President to fill a vacancy on a federal court and that, before confirmation, they must answer questions from the Senate Judiciary Committee. You may wish to present students with an example from an actual hearing. Have students complete the Chapter 18 Essential Question Essay on p. 156 in their *Essential Questions Journals.*

EXTEND THE LESSON ▬▬▬▬▬▬▬▬

L3 Differentiate Have students select one Supreme Court case and write an editorial explaining whether they agree or disagree with the Court's decision and why. Be sure that students include their judicial philosophy in their editorials.

TEACHER INSTRUCTIONS

PURPOSE

To help frame an answer to the ✪ **Essential Question:** *What should be the role of the judicial branch?*, students need to know the 1st Amendment freedoms and how courts must balance the freedoms of the individual with the common good of society.

LESSON GOALS

- Identify the federal protections and limits of 1st Amendment freedoms by completing a chart of 1st Amendment landmark cases.
- Learn how the 14th Amendment's Due Process Clause protects civil liberties from state and local government through teacher-led discussion.
- Explain 1st Amendment freedoms by creating a brochure.

MATERIALS

- ⊘ **Online Student Edition** and copies of ⊘ **Background Note 5.4,** located at PearsonSuccessNet.com
- *Essential Questions Journal*
- Copies of ⊘ **Activity 5.4,** *First Amendment Landmark Cases,* located at PearsonSuccessNet.com
- Copies of ⊘ **Assessment 5.4,** located at PearsonSuccessNet.com

BEFORE CLASS

Distribute copies of ⊘ **Background Note 5.4.** For more in-depth information, refer students to the ⊘ **Online Student Edition** Chapter 19. You may wish to have students read these materials before coming to class. You may also want students to complete the *Essential Questions Journal* Chapter 19 Warmup and Exploration, pp. 157–163, before class.

> **L2 Differentiate** Instead of students reading the Background Note on their own, have volunteers take turns reading portions aloud in class. After each portion is read, have a volunteer other than the reader summarize the information.

> **L2 Differentiate** Have students listen to the audio summary available at PearsonSuccessNet.com.

TEACH
DAY 1

1. Introduce the Lesson Inform students that a recent survey revealed that more Americans know the names of the five characters on the Simpsons television show than know the five 1st Amendment freedoms. Have students name the Simpsons (*Homer, Bart, Marge, Lisa, Maggie*) and then the 1st Amendment freedoms and rights (*freedoms of religion, speech, and press; right to assemble, right to petition the government for redress of grievances).* Ask: **Why do you think these rights are called "the unalienable rights"?** (*They cover the most basic of rights.*) **What additional rights, if any, would you consider unalienable?**

2. Discuss Background Note Ask students to scan ✪**Background Note 5.4** as they consider these questions: What does it mean to say that rights are relative, not absolute? (*Individuals can exercise their rights only as long as their actions do not infringe on the rights of others.*) From what or whom does the 14th Amendment protect citizens' rights? (*state governments*) Why does the Bill of Rights not protect citizens against the states? (*The Bill of Rights applies only to the federal government.*)

3. Define Key Terms and Phrases Write the following terms on the board and work with the class to agree on definitions: *civil liberties* (guarantees of the safety of persons, opinions, and property from arbitrary acts of government); *Bill of Rights* (the first ten amendments to the Constitution); *unalienable rights* (rights that cannot be taken away—life, liberty, and the pursuit of happiness); *Establishment Clause* (creates a "wall of separation between church and state" by prohibiting government from passing any law that establishes a state or national religion or favoring one religion over another); *Free Exercise Clause* (guarantees all people the right to believe whatever they choose in matters of religion). Have students copy the information into their notebooks.

> **L2 ELL Differentiate** Explain that the term *church* refers to all religions, and *state* refers to local, state, and national government.

4. Research Landmark Cases Have students work in pairs to complete the chart in ✪**Activity 5.4,** *First Amendment Landmark Cases,* by identifying the Court rulings on several 1st Amendment landmark cases. Direct them to use their ✪**Online Student Edition** or their textbook as references to help them complete the chart. Discuss the rulings as a class. Ask: **What can you conclude about the Court's reasoning in Establishment Clause cases (cases 1–5)?** (*Government must maintain strict neutrality, neither aiding nor opposing religion.*) **When is the free exercise of religion limited by the Court?** (*when the free exercise breaks a law, harms the safety of a person or community, or goes against public morals*) **Why is it important that government cannot censor speech or the press?** (*to allow all views, including unpopular ones, to be expressed*)

> **L2 Differentiate** Have pairs complete only the cases related to freedom of religion (1 through 9), and then complete the rest of the chart as a class.

> **L2 L3 Differentiate** Organize the class into groups of three students, then assign each group three of the cases on the chart. Each group should research only its assigned cases. Then have the groups reconvene as a class and teach one another the Court's rulings on their assigned cases.

> **L2 Differentiate** Provide students with the following list of Understandings. Ask them to match the 18 landmark cases to one or more of the Understandings.

- The Establishment Clause sets up "a wall of separation between church and state." *(cases 1–5)*
- The Free Exercise Clause protects religious beliefs but does not protect religious actions that violate laws or threaten safety. *(cases 6–9)*
- The guarantees of free speech and press are intended to protect the expression of unpopular views. *(cases 10–15)*
- The government cannot place prior restraint on spoken or written words. *(cases 10–12)*
- The rights of peaceable assembly and petition, basic to democracy, protect the people's right to bring their views to the attention of public officials. *(cases 16–18)*

DAY 2

5. *Create a "First Amendment Freedoms" Brochure* Have students use their knowledge about the unalienable rights to make a brochure titled "First Amendment Freedoms" for new immigrants. Underneath this title, ask them to write two subtitles: "Know Your Rights" and "Know Your Limits." You might wish to create a brochure ahead of time to provide an example to students. Then ask them to list or illustrate the rights and limits on freedom of religion, speech, press, assembly, and petition. In their brochures, students should list rights such as the right to peaceably assemble; the right to hold a demonstration in a public place; the right to voice opinions, even unpopular opinions; the right to symbolic speech, such as wearing armbands to protest war or burning the U.S. flag. Students' brochures should list limitations such as obtaining a permit before demonstrating; remaining peaceful during a protest; avoiding seditious speech; and avoiding libel or slander. Ask students to share their completed brochures at the end of class.

6. *Debrief* Have students return to the ***Essential Questions Journal*** Chapter 19 Warmup, p. 157, and reconsider their answers to part C.

7. *Assess* Distribute 🕖**Assessment 5.4,** in which students answer questions about 1st Amendment freedoms and the process of incorporation. Have students complete the Chapter 19 Essential Question Essay in their ***Essential Questions Journal,*** p. 165.

EXTEND THE LESSON ▬▬▬▬▬▬▬▬

L3 Differentiate Create a classroom Blogger Bulletin Board related to the issue of symbolic speech. Post the following statement on the bulletin board: "The United States needs a constitutional amendment making the burning of the American flag a crime." Choose two students with opposing points of view to post opinions about this statement on the bulletin board. Encourage other students to write their own reactions or responses to the original question or to student responses on notecards and post them on the board. Other possible 1st Amendment statements to "blog" may include: "Prayer should be allowed in public schools." or "Students should be allowed uncensored freedom of expression in school newspapers."

L4 Differentiate Have students create an illustrated "Know Your Rights" guide to the entire Bill of Rights that briefly explains what each right includes and the limits it puts on government. Students can use print or online resources to find examples of citizens exercising these rights.

L2 Differentiate Ask students to write a poem or song lyrics about 1st Amendment freedoms or one of the landmark cases from 🕖**Background Note 5.4** or 🕖**Activity 5.4.** Tell students to first summarize the case in their own words, including descriptive details. Then have them draft the poem or song lyrics, choosing their words carefully as they write.

SAMPLE POEM:

In *Gregory* v. *Chicago,* the crowd angrily erupted.

While the pelted protesters stayed calm, cool, collected.

Even so, off to jail the marchers were directed.

Oh no, said the Court. Peaceful protest is protected.

TEACHER INSTRUCTIONS

PURPOSE

To help students gain an understanding of civil rights in the United States, students are presented with a series of images and asked to determine how they would address the issue in an online interactive simulation.

LESSON GOALS

- Learn the evolution of civil rights in the United States by analyzing images.
- Compare and contrast past civil rights struggles with current and possible future ones.

MATERIALS

- ⓐ**Online Student Edition** and ⓐ**Online Interactive Decision Making,** located at PearsonSuccessNet.com
- *Essential Questions Journal*

BEFORE CLASS

Refer students to the ⓐ**Online Student Edition** Chapter 21, Sections 2 and 3. You may wish to have students read these materials before coming to class. You may also want students to complete the *Essential Questions Journal* Chapter 21 Warmup, p. 174, and Exploration, pp. 175–178.

TEACH

1. Introduce the Lesson Tell students that through an online decision-making activity they are going to explore the history of the civil rights struggles of three groups of Americans.

2. Complete the Activity Have students complete the online activity in class or assign the simulation as homework. NOTE: If you decide to give this as a homework assignment, conduct the debrief at the beginning of class and then continue with the next lesson plan.

3. Debrief Once students have completed the online simulation, lead a discussion about civil rights in the United States. Ask: **Why was the civil rights movement necessary?** *(because discriminatory laws and practices still existed in society that worked to deny equal rights; for example, poll taxes and intimidation limited the ability of African Americans to vote, and segregation in schools denied them equal access to education)* **What civil rights issues, if any, do you predict that future generations will face?** *(Answers will vary but might include issues about immigrants or other.)*

4. Assess Have students write 3–5 conclusions about civil rights based on the online activity. You may wish to have students share these conclusions in class and follow up with a discussion of how the interactivity helps provide an answer to the ⓠ **Essential Question:** *What should be the role of the judicial branch?* You may also want to have students complete the Chapter 21 Essential Question Essay on p. 180 in their *Essential Questions Journal.*

TEACHER INSTRUCTIONS

PURPOSE

To frame an answer to the ✪ **Essential Question:** *What should be the role of the judicial branch?,* students need to know what constitutional provisions guarantee rights to people accused of crimes, and how the courts uphold the judicial principal of "innocent until proven guilty."

LESSON GOALS

- Understand 4th Amendment guarantees against unreasonable search and seizure through class discussion.
- Identify the rights of people accused of crimes.
- Apply the knowledge of the rights of the accused by producing a short newscast.

MATERIALS

- ⊘**Online Student Edition** and copies of ⊘**Background Note 5.6,** located at PearsonSuccessNet.com
- *Essential Questions Journal*
- Copies of ⊘**Activity 5.6A,** *Due Process and Admissible Evidence,* located at PearsonSuccessNet.com
- Copies of ⊘**Activity 5.6B,** *Newscast Guidelines,* located at PearsonSuccessNet.com
- Copies of ⊘**Assessment 5.6,** located at PearsonSuccessNet.com

BEFORE CLASS

Distribute copies of ⊘**Background Note 5.6.** For more in-depth information, refer students to the ⊘**Online Student Edition** Chapter 20. You may wish to have students read these materials before coming to class. You may also want students to complete the *Essential Questions Journal* Chapter 20 Warmup, p. 166, before class.

L2 Differentiate Instead of students reading the Background Note on their own, guide a discussion of it by asking such questions as "What protections for the accused are included in the 6th Amendment?"

L2 Differentiate Have students listen to the audio summary available at PearsonSuccessNet.com.

L2 ELL Differentiate Have students underline difficult words in the Background Note and define these words as a class before you introduce the lesson.

TEACH

1. Introduce the Lesson Write "due process of law" on the board. Ask students what it means. (*Actions of government and law enforcement must be fair and follow established rules.*) Have students consider what might result from the following actions without fair laws or due process of law: someone criticizes the government (*banishment, execution*); shoplifting (*hand cut off, other torture—punishment exceeding the crime*); a suspect without an attorney is tried only by a judge, not by a jury (*sham trial with rigged witnesses*). Then ask: **What is the underlying principle for persons accused of crimes in the U.S. justice system?** (*People are innocent until proven guilty.*) **Who has the burden of proving guilt?** (*the prosecution or government*) Tell students that in this lesson, they will look at the rules and standards that the Supreme Court uses to examine the constitutional rights of the accused, as well as the responsibility of law enforcement to use proper procedures.

2. Discuss Background Note and Activity As a class, discuss **⚡Activity 5.6A** and go over **⚡Background Note 5.6,** which presents scenarios about due process, rules of evidence, and rights of the accused. Ask: **Were you surprised by any of the Court rulings? Which ones? Why?**

3. Prepare Newscasts Organize students into groups of three. Assign each group a landmark case from either **⚡Background Note 5.6** or **⚡Activity 5.6A** (exclusionary rule cases). Explain that each group will write a radio or TV newscast summarizing a landmark Supreme Court case concerning the rights of the accused. In character as a reporter and two interviewees (one for the defense and one for the prosecution), students should answer the questions *Who?, What?, When?, Where?, Why?,* and *How?* about their case in a 3-minute news story. You might want to ask students to research their case for homework.

Performance Rubric Explain that an excellent newscast will meet the following standards. *Planning:* The group made excellent use of planning time, sharing the writing and incorporating peer feedback. The selection of information used was well thought out and insightful. *Presentation:* The newscast was creative, interesting, organized, focused on the topic, and an appropriate length. Group members worked together harmoniously and dynamically. The dialogue was clear and flowed logically.

> **L2 Differentiate** Instead of creating a group newscast, have students write a short public-service announcement informing U.S. citizens of their rights if they are accused of a crime.

4. Present Newscasts Have the groups perform their newscasts. After each presentation, ask the rest of the class to peer assess the newscast in regard to the facts presented and its overall creativity.

5. Debrief Ask students whether they believe the Supreme Court has extended too many protections or not enough protections to the accused. Have them cite landmark cases as they offer their opinions.

6. Assess Distribute **⚡Assessment 5.6,** in which students diagram the due process rights of the accused. Have students complete the Chapter 20 Essential Question Essay on p. 173 in their *Essential Questions Journal.*

EXTEND THE LESSON

> **L3 Differentiate** Ask students to answer this question in a short essay: Why does a democracy need due process laws and procedures that define how government can use its power?

> **L4 Differentiate** Have students incorporate the majority, concurring, and dissenting opinions of the Court into their landmark-case newscast.

> **L2 Differentiate ELL** Have students draw an illustrated guide that shows which law enforcement actions are limited by the 4th Amendment, including rights against unreasonable searches and seizures and the exclusionary rule. Law enforcement actions that are upheld by Court rulings should also be included.

TEACHER INSTRUCTIONS

PURPOSE

To help frame an answer to the ⚙ **Essential Question:** *What should be the role of the judicial branch?,* students need to know how pretrial investigations, courtroom proceedings, and jury deliberations work together to administer justice according to law.

LESSON GOALS

- Apply information learned about due process, rules of evidence, and rights of the accused to a mock trial.
- Evaluate information, form arguments, and communicate effectively.

MATERIALS

- ⚙ **Background Note 5.7A,** *Order of Events,* located at PearsonSuccessNet.com (copies to all students)
- ⚙ **Background Note 5.7B,** *Attorney Guidelines,* located at PearsonSuccessNet.com (copies to attorneys)
- ⚙ **Activity 5.7A,** *Mock Trial Notes,* located at PearsonSuccessNet.com (copies to all students)
- ⚙ **Activity 5.7B,** *Police Officers' Report,* located at PearsonSuccessNet.com (copies to attorneys and police officer)
- ⚙ **Activity 5.7C,** *Juror Questionnaire,* located at PearsonSuccessNet.com (copies to all prospective jurors)
- ⚙ **Activity 5.7D,** *Search Warrant Application and Search Warrant,* located at PearsonSuccessNet.com (attorneys view before trial; possibly use during trial)
- **Trial 5.a:** *Newspaper Articles* (copies to all students or read aloud)
- **Trial 5.b:** *Exhibit A—Photos of destruction* (attorneys view before trial; may use during trial)
- **Trial 5.c:** *Exhibit B—Evidence* (attorneys view before trial; may use during trial)
- **Trial 5.d:** *Exhibit C—Photo taken with cell phone* (attorneys view before trial; may use during trial)
- **Trial 5.e:** *Map of Edgeville* (attorneys view before trial; may use during trial)
- **Trial: Role Cards 1–15** (Cut apart and distribute to assigned students. See Day 1, Step 3. Attorneys should also receive copies of witnesses' Role Cards, because these act as witness statements.)

BEFORE CLASS

Have students review ⊘**Activity 5.6A,** *Due Process and Admissible Evidence,* from the previous lesson. In addition, distribute copies of ⊘**Background Note 5.7A,** *Order of Events.* Have students read these materials before Day 1 of the mock trial simulation.

TEACH
DAY 1

1. Introduce the Lesson Distribute copies of ⊘**Activity 5.7A,** *Mock Trial Notes,* and ask students to brainstorm five principles of the judicial system. Discuss and guide their answers. Review ⊘**Activity 5.6A** from Lesson 5.6, which pertains to rights of the accused, due process, and types of evidence admissible in court. Then proceed with the activities below.

2. Introduce the Case Have student volunteers read aloud **Trial 5.a,** the two newspaper articles. Explain that the class will hold a criminal trial of the accused, Chris Jones.

3. Assign Roles The following assignments are recommended but can be adjusted to fit the number of students in your class: 1 judge, 4 defense attorneys, 4 prosecuting attorneys, 1 defendant, 3 witnesses for the prosecution, and 3 witnesses for the defense. (The arresting police officer may also be a witness.) Remaining students will fill out ⊘**Activity 5.7C,** *Juror Questionnaire* (see Step 6 below). Explain that attorneys will select jurors on Day 2 of the simulation. Students not selected as jurors may be named clerk, court recorder, and bailiff.

> **L3 Differentiate** Classrooms with a small number of students may reduce the number of attorneys for the prosecution and defense, as well as combine the roles of clerk, court recorder, and bailiff.

4. Discuss How Trials Unfold Go over ⊘**Background Note 5.7A,** *Order of Events,* which outlines the responsibilities of everyone in the trial as well as the chronological order in which events of the trial unfold.

> **L2 Differentiate** To help students see the alternating roles during a trial, have them highlight the defense's roles in one color and the prosecution's roles in a different color on the *Order of Events.*

5. Distribute Materials Distribute copies of the remaining **Activities, Background Notes,** and **Role Cards** to their specific recipients as noted in the "Materials" section. As homework, attorneys and their witnesses should familiarize themselves with their pertinent information.

6. Juror Questionnaire Have prospective jurors complete and return ⊘**Activity 5.7C,** *Juror Questionnaire.* Encourage students to fill out the questionnaire "in character." That is, some may be married with children, have been a crime victim, have been charged with a crime, or work in law enforcement in some capacity.

7. Conclude Day 1 Explain that on Day 2, attorneys and witnesses will begin to prepare their sides of the case. Caution students about the need for pretrial secrecy.

DAY 2

NOTE: Steps 1, 2, and 3 below should occur simultaneously.

1. Prepare Arguments and Witnesses Have attorneys and witnesses work in their groups to prepare their sides of the case. Be sure they analyze the evidence, witness statements (Role Cards), police notes, and so on, as listed on **⊘ Activity 5.7A,** *Mock Trial Notes.* The attorneys' Role Cards and **⊘ Background Note 5.7B,** *Attorney Guidelines,* explain additional attorney responsibilities, such as rehearsing direct examination testimony and practicing cross-examination testimony. Circulate among groups to provide direction and to prompt attorneys with clues if necessary. (See Answer Key for **⊘ Activity 5.7A,** *Mock Trial Notes.*)

2. Jury Selection Have an assistant attorney for each side hold jury selection by examining the *Juror Questionnaires* and interviewing each prospective juror. (Remind the jury that they must remain in character during the selection process, trial, and deliberations.) Jurors should rise and swear to answer truthfully the questions asked of them concerning their qualifications to act as a juror in the case.

> **L2 Differentiate** If assistant attorneys are struggling to develop questions for prospective jurors, provide them with prompts such as the following questions:
>
> - Do you know any of the parties involved in the case?
> - Can you be impartial?
> - I see that you [work in law enforcement/have a teenage child/have been a victim of a crime/have been charged with a misdemeanor/etc.]. How will this affect your judgment as a juror?
> - Would you be able to send an 18-year-old to jail for one year if he or she is found guilty of this crime?

3. Judge and Clerk The judge should study relevant information as noted on **Role Card 1.** The clerk may assist the judge in this task.

> **L2, L3, L4 Differentiate** If class time remains after jury selection (while the prosecution and defense teams collaborate with their clients and witnesses), assign jurors, the recorder, and the bailiff the following task: One of those accused in the mock crime was a juvenile. Explain the major differences between juvenile and adult court systems. Have students work in pairs or small groups to complete this assignment.

4. Conclude Day 2 Review **⊘ Background Note 5.7A,** *Order of Events,* which the class will follow in the Mock Trial on Day 3.

DAY 3

1. Hold the Trial When the defense and prosecution are ready, the case comes to trial. Arrange the classroom as shown in the diagram on the next page. Have students follow **⊘ Background Note 5.7A,** *Order of Events,* as they conduct the trial.

Court Layout

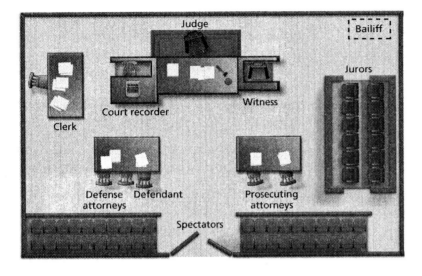

2. Debrief Conduct a post-trial debriefing. Ask the following questions:

- What were key points in the trial?
- Which basic principles of the judicial system were most in play during the trial?
- Which evidence was most convincing?
- What questions could have been asked that were not asked?
- Were jurors influenced by their emotions?
- Would you trust a jury of your peers to determine your guilt or innocence? Can you think of a better system of deciding innocence or guilt than a jury system?
- Are some parts of the trial more important than others?
- Did the system produce a fair verdict?
- Were there any aspects of the conduct of the trial or the law being applied that would be grounds for appealing this case to a higher court?

3. Assess Have students complete the Unit 5 Essential Question Essay Warmup, and then answer the 🅠 Essential Question: *What should be the role of the judicial branch?,* in their *Essential Questions Journal,* pp. 181–182.

EXTEND THE LESSON

L3 Differentiate Ask students who researched the juvenile system to explain what would happen to the 15-year-old in this case.

L3 Differentiate Have student attorneys continue in their roles to appeal the case to the appellate court of their judicial circuit.

L4 Differentiate Hold a trial about the 1st Amendment issue of free expression. Is the rally leader guilty of incitement? Did the rally leader's actions compel the other students to action? Does the Constitution protect speech at a rally or restrict it as a clear and present danger to the community?

UNIT 6

Comparative Political and Economic Systems

UNIT OVERVIEW

This group of lessons focuses on the purposes, types, and economic roles of government throughout history and in today's global economy. The lessons culminate in a classroom simulation in which students negotiate an international trade agreement. At the end of this unit, students will be able to craft an answer to the 🌐 **Essential Question:** *How should a government meet the needs of its people?* You may wish to have students begin their study by completing the *Essential Questions Journal* Unit 6 Warmup, p. 185.

UNIT GOALS

- Identify the purposes of government.
- Understand various forms of government.
- Explain how governments evolve from dictatorships to democracies.
- Understand how governments establish economic systems to meet citizens' needs.
- Determine the reasons nations trade and how their governments interact in the global economy.

TIME ALLOTMENT

This unit of activities is intended to be taught in 10 days (or 5 days on a block schedule).

DAY 1	Lesson 1	The Purposes of Government
DAY 2	Lesson 2	Systems of Government
DAY 3	Lesson 3	Transitions to Democracy
DAY 4	Lesson 4	Economic and Political Systems
DAY 5	Lesson 5	The U.S. Government and the Global Economy
DAY 6	Lesson 6	Interactive Decision-Making: Diplomacy
DAYS 7–8	Lesson 7	Trade Negotiation

ENDURING UNDERSTANDINGS

- Governments are organized according to a variety of principles.
- *Sovereignty* is the ultimate authority to make decisions and maintain order.
- All democracies are based on popular sovereignty, or rule by the people.
- All governments claim to be the legitimate representative of their people's interests and fulfill this claim with varying degrees of sincerity and success.
- Democracy takes root when competing groups agree to compromise and cooperate to make government work.
- Economic freedom demands political freedom, and vice versa.
- Governments should pursue economic policies that serve national self-interest and that are politically achievable.
- International trade binds countries together to mutual benefit.

UNIT 6

LESSON 1

The Purposes of Government

TEACHER INSTRUCTIONS

PURPOSE

To frame an answer to the ⊕ **Essential Question:** *How should a government meet the needs of its people?,* students need to understand the principles and ideas underlying democratic government in the United States and the world.

LESSON GOALS

- Create a concept web to define why governments are needed.
- Understand that popular sovereignty is the voice of the people in their government.
- Identify the concept of legitimacy in the Declaration of Independence and explain why it is important to governments.

MATERIALS

- ⊘**Online Student Edition** and copies of ⊘**Background Note 6.1,** located at PearsonSuccessNet.com
- *Essential Questions Journal*
- Copies of ⊘**Activity 6.1,** *Analyzing the Declaration of Independence,* located at PearsonSuccessNet.com
- Copies of ⊘**Assessment 6.1,** located at PearsonSuccessNet.com

BEFORE CLASS

Distribute copies of ⊘**Background Note 6.1.** For more in-depth information, refer students to the ⊘**Online Student Edition,** Chapter 22, Section 1. You may wish to have students read these materials before coming to class. You may also want students to complete the *Essential Questions Journal,* Unit 6 Warmup, p. 185, if they haven't already done so, and Chapter 22 Warmup, p. 186, before class.

> **L2 Differentiate** Instead of students reading the Background Note on their own, have volunteers take turns reading portions aloud in class. After each portion is read, have a volunteer other than the reader summarize the information.

> **L2 Differentiate** Have students listen to the online summary available at PearsonSuccessNet.com

TEACH

1. Activate Prior Knowledge Tell students that the goal of this unit is to explore the ⊕ **Essential Question:** *How should a government meet the needs of its people?* To help them start thinking about this question, have them take out the *Essential Questions Journal* Unit 6 Warmup, Part A, p. 185, where they listed responsibilities they think government should fulfill, or have them complete the assignment in class. Then, on the board, create a class concept web with students' ideas from the *Journal* activity. Have students vote to rank the three most important responsibilities they think government should have.

> **L2 Differentiate** If students have trouble coming up with items for the list, ask them to think about the government services they see around them every day, such as police and fire protection, public schools, road maintenance and repair, and so on.

2. Introduce the Lesson Tell students that in this lesson they will discuss the reasons governments exist and the source of government's power. Begin by asking: **Is government necessary?** Discuss students' ideas about why we, and they, need government and what its functions are in meeting citizens' needs. Then ask: **What is *popular sovereignty?*** Explain that the word *popular* has the same Latin root as *people,* and that *sovereignty* describes a country's rights to self-government. Explain that when government is controlled by the people, directly or through representatives, this is known as popular sovereignty. Next, ask: **What is *legitimacy?*** Explain that the root of *legitimacy* comes from the Latin word *lex,* which means "law." Ask students how this might relate to the meaning of *legitimacy.* (*Legitimacy is literally "legal rule."*) Clarify that *legitimacy* is the right to rule. Tell students that even a government that rules by force seeks legitimacy. Ask: **Why is legitimacy important to a government?** *(The government will be more stable and likely to last if the people believe it has the right to rule them.)* What is the basis of the U.S. government's legitimacy? *(It is based on written law.)*

> **L2 Differentiate ELL** Write "popular sovereignty" and "legitimacy" on the board. Pronounce both terms for students and then ask them to use each term in a sentence.

3. Complete the Activity Distribute copies of ✪**Activity 6.1,** *Analyzing the Declaration of Independence.* Tell students that they will read the excerpts from the Declaration and analyze them to identify phrases that support the loss of Britain's legitimacy to rule the American colonies and the gain of legitimacy for the new government.

> **L2 Differentiate** Read through the worksheet excerpts as a class. Pause after reading each paragraph to have students identify phrases concerning the right to rule and restate the phrases in their own words.

> **L4 Differentiate** Have students read the full Declaration of Independence reproduced in their ✪**Online Student Edition** and write their summaries based on the entire document.

4. Debrief Wrap up this activity by asking students if they think the Declaration makes the colonists' case that Britain had lost the right to rule the colonies. Make reference to the concepts of popular sovereignty and legitimacy discussed earlier. Have volunteers read their summaries aloud. Then create a class concept web that summarizes the arguments of the colonists against Britain's rule.

5. Assess Distribute ✪**Assessment 6.1,** which asks students to answer questions about main concepts of this lesson.

EXTEND THE LESSON ▬▬▬▬▬

> **L3 Differentiate** Have students collect images and text from magazines or the Internet to create posters that address the question: Why do we have government? Display finished posters around the classroom.

> **L4 Differentiate** Have students create a PowerPoint presentation that explains their ideas about why government is or is not necessary. Presentations should include specific examples to support students' ideas. Ask students to include how important they think it is that government meets or does not meet its people's needs.

UNIT 6
LESSON
2

TEACHER INSTRUCTIONS

PURPOSE

To frame an answer to the ❸ **Essential Question:** *How should a government meet the needs of its people?,* students need to compare and contrast the purposes, structures, and functions of government systems.

LESSON GOALS

- Compare and contrast parliamentary and federal systems of government.
- Understand the features of totalitarian governments (communist, fascist, theocratic).
- Evaluate the levels of democracy and government control in different government systems.

MATERIALS

- ⦿**Online Student Edition** and copies of the ⦿**Background Note 6.2,** located at PearsonSuccessNet.com
- *Essential Questions Journal*
- *American Government Essential Questions Video* DVD or ⦿ online at PearsonSuccessNet.com
- Copies of ⦿**Activity 6.2,** *Government Systems Fact Game,* located at PearsonSuccessNet.com
- Index cards (4–5 per student, plus 2 for each of 2–4 teams)
- Internet access
- Copies of ⦿**Assessment 6.2,** located at PearsonSuccessNet.com

BEFORE CLASS

Distribute copies of ⦿**Background Note 6.2.** For more in-depth information, refer students to the ⦿**Online Student Edition,** Chapter 22, Section 4, and Chapter 23, Section 2. You may wish to have students read these materials before coming to class. You may also want students to complete the *Essential Questions Journal,* Chapter 22 Exploration II, p. 188, before class.

> **L2 Differentiate** Ask students to read aloud and define the boldface terms in the Background Note. Then have volunteers explain why these terms are important for understanding the information.

> **L2 Differentiate** Have students listen to the audio summary located at PearsonSuccessNet.com.

TEACH

1. Introduce the Lesson Tell students that in this lesson they will discuss the structures and features of different types of governments. Draw a concept web on the board titled "Systems of Government," with two subordinate ovals labeled "Democratic" and "Totalitarian." With students, list features of parliamentary and federal systems under "Democratic," and of communist, fascist, and theocratic systems under "Totalitarian." Clarify that a parliamentary government has a prime minister who is the leader of the party with the majority in the legislature, and who is not elected directly by the people. Explain that the executive branch is drawn from the legislative branch. In this system, a president, premier, or monarch takes a mostly symbolic role as the chief of state. In a presidential system like the United States, the President is the chief of state as well as the head of the executive branch. Then show students the *American Government Essential Questions Video* for Unit 6, which illustrates how governments function in the United Kingdom, China, Mexico, and other countries. Direct students to pay attention to differences and similarities among the countries profiled, and discuss the questions that follow.

> **L2 Differentiate** Clarify that *totalitarian* describes a government that is a dictatorship, ruled by one person or one party, and does not allow any dissent. In other words, a totalitarian government has *total* control over the nation.

> **L2 Differentiate ELL** Ask for volunteers to describe the form of government of their countries of origin. Discuss how these governments are similar to and different from the government of the United States and the countries profiled in the video.

2. Complete the Activity Distribute ⊘Activity 6.2, *Government Systems Fact Game.* Tell students they will follow directions on the worksheet to play a fact game. Each question will cover a fact about a type of government system or a specific nation's system, such as a question about some aspect of the U.S. federal and presidential system. Point out that some facts may describe the government of more than one nation. In these cases, the answer should include all nations to which the fact applies. Questions should be based on their ⊘**Online Student Edition,** ⊘**Background Note 6.2,** and Internet research. Organize the class into two or four teams of four to five students each. Provide 22 index cards to each team. This will give each team two cards to label categories and four or five cards per student to write questions. After the teams create and arrange their game cards, pair teams to play.

3. Debrief To wrap up the lesson, draw a horizontal line across the board. Label the left end "Freedom" and the right end "Government Control." Discuss how the different systems of government make decisions and consider the rights and welfare of citizens. Then ask students, as a class, to position each of the following systems on this continuum on the board between total freedom and total government control: federal republic (U.S., Mexico), parliamentary democracy (UK, Japan), communist government (Cuba, former USSR), fascist government (Nazi Germany), and theocracy (Iran). Have students give reasons for each placement.

4. Assess Distribute ⊘Assessment 6.2, which asks students to rate different systems of government and answer questions.

EXTEND THE LESSON

> **L3 Differentiate** Have students write a paragraph explaining whether they think it is best for the legislative branch of a government to have more power, for the executive branch to have more power, or for all three branches to have equal power, and why, using the UK and Mexico as examples.

> **L4 Differentiate** Mexico and the UK have recently made changes that have increased levels of democracy: the advent of free and fair elections in Mexico and Britain's reform of the House of Lords and devolution of powers to Scotland and Wales. Have students research and write an essay on the conditions and pressures that led to these changes in each country. Encourage them to draw conclusions about lessons other democracies might learn from these examples.

TEACHER INSTRUCTIONS

PURPOSE

To help frame an answer to the ✷ **Essential Question:** *How should a government meet the needs of its people?,* students need to be able to compare and contrast the purposes, structures, and functions of government systems and the ways in which governments participate in the national and global economy.

LESSON GOALS

- Understand the challenges of democratic transitions.
- Complete a chart listing the factors contributing to greater democracy and to failed democracy.
- Analyze the factors that might cause certain states to succeed or fail in their transitions to democracy by studying the examples of Iraq and Haiti.

MATERIALS

- ⦿ **Online Student Edition** and copies of ⦿ **Background Note 6.3,** located at PearsonSuccessNet.com
- *Essential Questions Journal*
- Copies of ⦿ **Activity 6.3,** *Evaluate Transitions to Democracy,* located at PearsonSuccessNet.com
- Internet access
- Copies of ⦿ **Assessment 6.3,** located at PearsonSuccessNet.com

BEFORE CLASS

Distribute copies of ⦿ **Background Note 6.3.** For more in-depth information, refer students to the ⦿ **Online Student Edition,** Chapter 22, Section 3. You may wish to have students read these materials before coming to class. You may also want students to complete the *Essential Questions Journal,* Chapter 22 Exploration III, p. 189, before class.

> **L2 Differentiate** Guide a discussion of the Background Note by asking questions, such as **What is the difference between a democracy and a republic?** and **Is pure democracy an effective form of government?**

> **L2 Differentiate** Have student listen to the audio summary available at PearsonSuccessNet.com.

TEACH

1. Introduce the Lesson Explain that this lesson is about transition from one type of government to another—to a more democratic government—and the challenges nations face when they attempt this change. Ask: **How can a transition from dictatorship or colonial rule to democracy be difficult, even though it is a positive development?** *(Sample response: More freedom means more responsibility. Citizens in a democracy need to participate, by taking responsibility for voting and overseeing the acts of their government, and to think for themselves.)* Draw a two-column chart on the board. Label the columns "Success" and "Failure." Have students offer answers to these questions to fill in the chart: **What factors lead to more democracy?** *(push for popular sovereignty, clashes between hard-liners and soft-liners, strong leaders of democratic movements, free press, multiple parties, civilian control over the military, interest groups, economic opportunities, professional civil service, common trust among citizens)* **What factors lead to the failure of democracy?** *(civil war, distrust, competition among groups for power, ethnic violence, independent and powerful military, no history of free institutions, weak economy)*

> **L2 Differentiate ELL** Clarify that a transition is a process involving major change.

> **L2 Differentiate ELL** Ask whether any students come from a country in transition and invite them to share their experiences.

2. Complete the Activity Distribute ⊘**Activity 6.3,** *Evaluate Transitions to Democracy.* Tell students that they will complete the chart on the worksheet to list factors that they think could lead to the success of democratization and factors that could lead to failure in Haiti and Iraq. Allow students time (or assign as homework) to research more details about the current situation in these countries relating to factors necessary to democratic consolidation.

> **L4 Differentiate** Suggest that students also evaluate an example of a failed state, such as Somalia or Afghanistan in the 1990s. They should list the factors that caused the failure of the government and then make recommendations for steps that nation should take to become more democratic.

3. Debrief To wrap up the lesson, review students' work on **Activity 6.3** as a class. Discuss which factors students thought might help Haiti and Iraq be successful in their transitions to democracy and which factors they thought could cause them to fail. Ask students if, ultimately, they think that Haiti and Iraq will succeed in their transitions to democracy.

4. Assess Distribute ⊘**Assessment 6.3,** which asks students questions about transitions to democracy.

EXTEND THE LESSON

> **L3 Differentiate** Organize students into four groups and assign each group one of the following: Czechoslovakia, Romania, Poland, and the Soviet Union. Have students in each group research and create a large flowchart showing how the country became communist, how the communist government maintained control, and how the communist government ended. Have them illustrate the flowchart with art, clippings from magazines, or Internet printouts.

> **L2 Differentiate** Have students research and prepare a short illustrated booklet for younger students on a person who influenced a change from communism to democracy, such as Lech Walesa, Vaclav Havel, Alexander Solzhenitsyn, or Pope John Paul II.

> **L4 Differentiate** Organize students into an even number of small teams. Assign equal numbers of teams to debate for and against the idea that one country can export democracy to another country. Have pairs of teams take turns debating. Then poll the class on which arguments were the best and whether the debate changed anyone's mind.

TEACHER INSTRUCTIONS

PURPOSE

To frame an answer to the ❸ **Essential Question:** *How should a government meet the needs of its people?*, students need to be able to compare and contrast economic systems in terms of how they meet the needs of a country and its people.

LESSON GOALS

- Understand the theories of Karl Marx by reviewing the main ideas of Marxism.
- Compare and contrast the effects of different economic systems on daily life.
- Role-play to understand the relationship between political and economic freedom.

MATERIALS

- ❼ **Online Student Edition** and copies of the ❼ **Background Note 6.4,** located at PearsonSuccessNet.com
- *Essential Questions Journal*
- Copies of ❼ **Activity 6.4,** *Comparing Life Under Capitalism and Communism,* located at PearsonSuccessNet.com
- Copies of ❼ **Assessment 6.4,** located at PearsonSuccessNet.com

BEFORE CLASS

Distribute copies of ❼ **Background Note 6.4.** For more in-depth information, refer students to the ❼ **Online Student Edition,** Chapter 23, Section 2. You may wish to have students read these materials before coming to class. You may also want students to complete the *Essential Questions Journal,* Chapter 23 Warmup, p. 192, and Chapter 23, Exploration II, p. 194, before class.

> **L2 Differentiate** Instead of students reading the Background Note on their own, have volunteers take turns reading portions aloud in class. After each portion is read, have a volunteer other than the reader summarize the information.

> **L2 Differentiate** Have students listen to the audio summary available at PearsonSuccessNet.com.

TEACH

1. Introduce the Lesson Explain that this lesson is about how different types of government manage a nation's economy. Share that, in addition to capitalism, there are two other main economic systems: socialism and communism. Remind students that they learned about the political features of these two systems in Lesson 2. Both systems developed from ideas of economist and philosopher Karl Marx (1818–1883) and his colleague and writing partner, Friedrich Engels (1820–1895), based on their analysis of the terrible working conditions under capitalism at the birth of the Industrial Revolution. With students, list the four main Marxist concepts on the board and discuss each one—the history of the class struggle, the Labor Theory of value, the role of institutions, and the dictatorship of the proletariat.

L2 Differentiate ELL Explain that *Marxism* and *communism* are sometimes used to mean the same thing, although more correctly *Marxism* is a body of thought, while *communism* is the political and economic system based on that thought. Pronounce and define *proletariat* (working-class people).

2. Complete the Activity Tell students that they will now consider what living under communism might be like and how it might compare to daily life under capitalism. Pair students and distribute ✪ **Activity 6.4,** *Comparing Life Under Capitalism and Communism.* Tell students that they will take a specific role with a partner to develop ideas of what life might be like under capitalism and communism. Then they will write a dialogue about daily life under these systems. Explain that partners must both play the same role, but one will choose to write about capitalism and the other about communism.

L2 Differentiate ELL Assign more straightforward role, such as farmer or restaurant server. If students have trouble with writing the dialogue, have them create a list of key points that they can use to tell their stories to partners. They may also tell their stories in illustrated panels or sketches.

3. Debrief When students have completed their dialogues, draw a Venn diagram on the board in which students list features of life under each system. Discuss with students what they learned from this activity. What are some positive and negative features about each system?

4. Assess Distribute ✪ **Assessment 6.4,** which asks students to write a summary comparing and contrasting capitalism and communism based on the ✪ **Essential Question** and to evaluate these systems along a continuum of political and economic freedom.

EXTEND THE LESSON

L3 Differentiate Instruct students to do research to create an in-depth report comparing and contrasting economic facts about the United States with one socialist country, such as Sweden, and one communist country, such as China or North Korea. Facts might include GDP, literacy rate, mortality, average work week, vacation time, income, national tax rates, and so on. Encourage students to arrange some of the data in the form of graphs or tables. Tell students to complete the assignment with a written summary that draws conclusions about how well each nation meets the needs of its citizens.

L2 Differentiate Provide students with a blank world map and a world atlas or current country map to share. Have them identify the five remaining Communist nations—China, Cuba, Vietnam, Laos, North Korea—on the atlas or country map. Then ask them to locate these countries on the blank map, label them, create a map key for "Communist States" and "Capitalist States," and color the map accordingly.

TEACHER INSTRUCTIONS

PURPOSE

To frame an answer to the 🌐 **Essential Question:** *How should a government meet the needs of its people?,* students need to understand how global trade works and how the United States participates in the global economy.

LESSON GOALS

- Understand why nations trade by relating trade to purchases made by students.
- Explain the role of the U.S. government in the global economy and study different perspectives on NAFTA.
- Determine the current status of U.S. participation in an international organization or trade agreement.

MATERIALS

- ⦿ **Online Student Edition** and copies of ⦿ **Background Note 6.5,** located at PearsonSuccessNet.com
- *Essential Questions Journal*
- Copies of ⦿ **Activity 6.5,** *The United States and NAFTA,* located at PearsonSuccessNet.com
- Copies of ⦿ **Assessment 6.5,** located at PearsonSuccessNet.com

BEFORE CLASS

Distribute copies of ⦿ **Background Note 6.5.** For more in-depth information, refer students to the ⦿ **Online Student Edition,** Chapter 23, Section 3. You may wish to have students read these materials before coming to class. You may also want students to complete the *Essential Questions Journal,* Chapter 23, Exploration III, p. 195, before class.

> **L2 Differentiate** Help students create an outline of the Background Note by identifying the main idea and supporting details. Write the outline on the board.

> **L2 Differentiate** Have students listen to the audio summary available at PearsonSuccessNet.com.

TEACH

1. Introduce the Lesson Explain that this lesson is about globalization and why nations trade. Explain that trade is an exchange of goods and services that allows trading partners to achieve higher levels of efficiency. Have students suggest items they have bought recently that came from another country. Ask why that good might be imported instead of having been produced in the United States. Encourage students to see that trade allows nations to specialize in producing goods and services based on local materials and skills. Tell students that countries, businesses, and individuals are all part of a global economy that affects everyone and is governed by international institutions, trade agreements, and national governments. Take a vote to find out how many students think globalization is a positive development and how many think it is more harmful to the United States than helpful. Ask volunteers to explain their reasoning.

> **L2 Differentiate ELL** Pronounce and write the definition of *globalization* on the board.

2. Complete the Activity Distribute ❷Activity 6.5, *The United States and NAFTA*. Have students read about NAFTA in their ❷Online Student Editions and complete the chart with positive and negative effects that NAFTA has had on each group. If students have access to the Internet, direct them to resources providing different perspectives on NAFTA. Sources may include Web sites produced by members of Congress, labor unions, pro-business groups such as the U.S. Chamber of Commerce, respected think tanks, and newspaper editorial pages. You may wish students to complete this research for homework.

> **L2 Differentiate** Before beginning this activity, have students read through each group listed and explain what they do in the economy.

3. Debrief When students have completed their research and summaries, ask them to vote again to indicate if they think globalization is a positive or harmful development for Americans. If the count is different than it was earlier, ask students who changed their minds why they did so. Ask students regardless of whether they changed their minds what information they found that most strongly supported their opinion. Have students share that information with the class.

4. Assess Distribute ❷Assessment 6.5, which asks students to think about aspects of international trade and globalization and to write a brief essay summarizing whether or not they think the U.S. government's participation in the global economy helps to meet its citizens' needs.

EXTEND THE LESSON

> **L3 Differentiate** Ask students to do research and create a circle graph showing what nations the United States is most dependent on for petroleum and what percentage of U.S. oil comes from each nation. Have students write a summary about how this relationship might affect U.S. relations and policy with these nations.

> **L2 Differentiate ELL** Have students work in pairs or small groups to create an informational poster or brochure about one of the international organizations to which the United States belongs, such as the World Trade Organization or the World Bank. Have students present their work to the class.

> **L4 Differentiate** Have students use the library or Internet news sources to locate three to five news reports about current U.S. participation in one international organization or one international trade agreement. Have students summarize the status of U.S. participation in that organization and explain what this may mean for the U.S. economy in the future.

UNIT 6

LESSON 6

Interactive Decision Making: Diplomacy

TEACHER INSTRUCTIONS

PURPOSE
To help students gain an understanding of the complexity of international relations, students will be presented with several scenarios in which they are the leader of a country making decisions about how best to proceed.

LESSON GOALS
- Learn the complexity of international relations by participating in and analyzing scenarios in an online interactive simulation.
- Identify the variables that can influence leaders to make different decisions even when they are confronted with the same circumstances.

MATERIALS
- ⊘ **Online Interactive Decision Making,** located at PearsonSuccessNet.com
- ⊘ **Online Student Edition**

BEFORE CLASS
Refer students to the ⊘ **Online Student Edition** Chapter 22, Sections 3 and 4. You may wish to have students read these materials before coming to class.

TEACH

1. Introduce the Lesson Tell students that through an online simulation they are going to explore the complexity of decision making in international relations.

2. Complete the Activity Have students complete the online activity in class or assign the simulation as homework. NOTE: If you decide to give this as a homework assignment, conduct the debrief at the beginning of class and then continue with the next day's lesson plan.

3. Debrief Once students have completed the online simulation, lead a discussion about the activity and students' thoughts about international relations. Ask: **What did you learn about the various ways nations might respond to a situation?** *(Students might say that it is a complex matter and is variable, depending on what the other parties decide or how they act.)* **What factors do you think play the most critical role in the decision-making process of a nation's leader?** *(Students might suggest national security, economic stability, domestic tranquility, political career, or relations with other nations.)*

4. Assess Have students write 3–5 conclusions about international relations. Follow up with a discussion of how the interactivity helps provide an answer to the ⓠ **Essential Question:** *How should a government meet the needs of its people?*

UNIT 6

LESSON

7

Trade Negotiation

PURPOSE

To frame an answer to the 🌎 **Essential Question: *How should a government meet the needs of its people?*,** students will conduct a Trade Negotiation simulation in which they must apply the information learned throughout this unit to determine how representatives of different forms of government might negotiate in the global market to achieve the goals of their nations.

LESSON GOALS

- Apply knowledge about different forms of government and economic systems.
- Learn how nations compete and leaders try to meet the needs of citizens in the global market.
- Evaluate and synthesize information, make decisions, and demonstrate reasoned judgment.

MATERIALS

- 📄 **Online Student Edition** and copies of 📄 **Background Notes 6.7A, 6.7B, 6.7C,** and **6.7D,** located at PearsonSuccessNet.com
- ***Essential Questions Journal***
- **Trade 6.a:** *World Political Map*
- **Trade: Role Cards 1–12** (Cut apart and distribute to assigned students.)
- 📄 **Activity 6.7,** *Goals Worksheet,* located at PearsonSuccessNet.com
- Internet access

BEFORE CLASS

For the simulation, organize students into four groups of three or more according to the roles on the Role Cards, so that each group of three represents one of the four nations: Mexico, the UK, China, and Nigeria. (You may assign specific roles to each student or let group members determine roles within each group. See note below regarding assigning roles according to student ability levels.) If more than 12 students are participating in the simulation, print or copy enough Role Cards for all groups. Post the world map **(Trade 6.a).** Point out the data presented on the map for each group. Tell students to note this information. Give each group time to research more about their roles and about the economic and political system of the nation they will represent. You may wish to assign this research for homework.

TEACH

1. Introduce the Lesson Explain that this activity—a Trade Negotiation—will give students insight into and understanding of how governments compete to buy and sell resources according to national goals and citizens' needs. Provide the country-appropriate 📄 **Background Note** to each group. Tell students that they will be role-playing a member of a delegation from their assigned nation. The goal of Mexico and Nigeria is to make a deal to sell oil to China and the UK. The goal of China and the UK is to make a deal to buy oil from either Mexico or Nigeria. Essentially, Mexico and Nigeria are seeking investment from China and the UK, while China and the UK are competing to buy oil from Mexico and Nigeria. Discuss the map and students' roles, and answer students' questions about the activity scenario. The Energy Information Administration's Web site publishes Country Energy Profiles, with detailed current information on the energy industry in each country, that you may wish to provide to students.

L2 Differentiate ELL Suggest that students identify any words on the map or Role Cards that they do not understand. After they have looked the words up in a dictionary, have them reread the materials with their definitions close at hand.

L4 Differentiate Have students research agreements the United States has made for importing or exporting petroleum with another nation or with OPEC. What did the United States promise to the other nation or to OPEC? What did the other side promise?

DAY 1

1. Delegations Establish Goals After students have had some time to review all the materials and think about their roles, distribute ⓐ Activity 6.7, *Goals Worksheet*. Have students from each nation now meet in their own group to discuss and establish at least three goals. They should discuss what they need to achieve in any agreement and what they can offer in exchange to meet their goals. Students should use the *Goals Worksheet* to list and describe their goals. Remind students that one goal of negotiations is to know what the other nation wants or needs, and to maintain a close balance of trade with the trade partner.

2. Delegations Meet: Round 1 The Mexican delegation meets with China's delegation, while the Nigerian delegation meets with the UK delegation. Groups exchange information and establish some preliminary ideas of what each wants and will give in return. Sellers lay out their terms; buyers respond to meet them or not. Then groups change so that Mexico meets with the UK and Nigeria with China. Tell students to remember that two nations are competing to sell, and two to buy petroleum.

3. Review the Status National delegations again meet within their own groups to discuss what they learned in the first round of the negotiations. They should review their *Goals Worksheet* and consider questions such as: Can we meet the terms of the other nation(s)? Do we have more to offer? Will the terms be satisfactory or not? Students should also consider what each group of buyers can do to reach an agreement and if sellers are satisfied or unsatisfied with the offers in the first round of the summit.

4. Delegations Meet: Round 2—Make a Preliminary Agreement Have students repeat the round of meetings from Step 2 to finalize an agreement with at least one nation. Both groups will record the agreed-upon terms or decide there will be no agreement. Agreements can be with one or both of the opposite groups. One copy of the agreement terms should be prepared and signed by both delegations.

DAY 2

1. Debrief Have groups report to the class as a whole on the preliminary agreement(s) they made. In what ways do they feel that the negotiation was a success for their nation? In what ways, if any, was it not? Discuss with students what they feel was the most challenging part of the summit for them, and how they met that challenge. Then have students each write a report summarizing the experience, stating the terms they reached or did not reach, and evaluating how well they feel their delegation met its goals.

L4 Differentiate Have students make a list of questions for another delegation—either one they could not negotiate with or one they competed with. Have the delegations answer them in an open-forum, whole-class format.

2. Assess Have students answer the **Essential Question:** *How should a government meet the needs of its people?* in their *Essential Questions Journal.* You may also use one of the following formats:

>   **Assessment option 1: Present answer in an essay.**

>   **Assessment option 2: Present answer in a multimedia format.**

>   **Assessment option 3: Present answer in a visual format.**

3. Conclude Point out that, through this Trade Negotiation, students should have gained a better understanding of what types of choices national governments make based on the goals of the government itself, and also on the needs of citizens. In trade negotiations, the delegation must consider how to get the best "deal" for citizens while maintaining the principles and laws of its own government.

EXTEND THE LESSON

L3 Differentiate Have students research to write a report on what agreements the United States has made for importing or exporting petroleum with another nation or with OPEC. Alternatively, students could investigate and report on any international trade agreement.

L2 Differentiate Ask students to find a recent news report about some agreement or group, such as the WTO or World Bank, to which the United States belongs. Students should then summarize the main ideas of the report in their own words.

L4 Differentiate Have students create a multimedia presentation on the future of global trade, including data on current trends. They should include predictions for both the near (5 years) and more distant (10–15 years) future.

UNIT 7 — Participating in State and Local Government

UNIT OVERVIEW

This group of lessons focuses on state and local government, including structures, duties and responsibilities, powers, services, and revenue and spending at the state and local levels. The lessons culminate in a classroom simulation of participation in state and local government in response to a dilemma in local economic development. At the end of this unit, students will be able to craft an answer to the **✪ Essential Question:** *What is the right balance of local, state, and federal government?*

UNIT GOALS

- Identify the main powers and purposes of state and local governments.
- Describe the organization and structure of state and local governments.
- Explain which level of government provides various types of services and why.
- Explain how states raise revenue through taxes and other methods.
- Identify the role of citizens in the passage of state and local legislation.
- Explain how citizens can participate in state and local government.

TIME ALLOTMENT

This unit of activities is intended to be taught in 10 days (or 5 days on a block schedule). The following time frame will help you plan your instruction.

DAY 1–2	Lesson 1	Introduction to State Government
DAY 3	Lesson 2	The Structure and Functions of State and Local Governments
DAY 4	Lesson 3	State and Local Services
DAY 5	Lesson 4	State Revenue and Spending
DAY 6	Lesson 5	Direct Democracy
DAY 7	Lesson 6	Interactive Decision Making: Your State and Local Government
DAY 8–10	Lesson 7	Participating in State and Local Government

ENDURING UNDERSTANDINGS

- Every state has a written constitution that defines the state's government.
- Most state governments have a constitutional separation of powers similar to the federal government, but the organization and processes of state governments vary from state to state.
- The U.S. Constitution reserves for the states all powers not delegated to the federal government or denied to the states. The most important of these powers is the police power.
- State and local governments are closest to the citizen and deliver many of the services that affect daily life.
- Sources of state and local funding include taxes, nontax sources, and borrowing.
- Individual citizens can participate directly in state and local government more readily than in the federal government.

TEACHER INSTRUCTIONS

PURPOSE

To frame an answer to the ✪ **Essential Question:** *What is the right balance of local, state, and federal government?,* students need to understand the purposes of state and local governments in the United States as defined by state constitutions.

LESSON GOALS

- Discuss and analyze a video showing ways to participate in state and local government.
- Examine the origins, features, and purposes of state constitutions through discussion of their six main principles.
- Analyze students' own state constitution and complete a chart identifying how it meets the six main principles.
- Explain federalism and the different roles of the federal and state governments.

MATERIALS

- ✪**Online Student Edition** and copies of ✪**Background Notes 7.1 A** and **7.1 B,** located at PearsonSuccessNet.com
- *Essential Questions Journal*
- *American Government: Experience It!* DVD or ✪ online at PearsonSuccessNet.com
- Copies of ✪**Activity 7.1,** *Analyzing Your State's Constitution,* located at PearsonSuccessNet.com
- Copies of ✪**Assessment 7.1,** located at PearsonSuccessNet.com
- Copies of your state constitution

DAY 1
BEFORE CLASS

Distribute copies of ✪**Background Notes 7.1 A** and **7.1 B.** For more in-depth information, refer students to the ✪**Online Student Edition,** Chapter 24, Section 1. You may wish to have students read these materials before coming to class. You may also want students to complete the *Essential Questions Journal,* Unit 7 Warmup, p. 202, and Chapter 24 Exploration, p. 204, before class.

> **L2 Differentiate** Work with students to define the boldfaced terms on ✪**Background Note 7.1A.** Be sure that they understand the concept of federalism. Explain any unfamiliar vocabulary in ✪**Background Note 7.1B** and ask students to describe the six principles in their own words.

> **L2 Differentiate** Have students listen to the audio summary located at PearsonSuccessNet.com

TEACH

1. Activate Prior Knowledge Tell students that the goal of this unit is to explore the
 Essential Question: *What is the right balance of local, state, and federal government?*
To help them start thinking about this question, have students take out the ***Essential Questions
Journal*** Unit Warmup, p. 202, where they listed the levels of government under which they live
and assigned different roles to each (or have them complete the assignment in class). On the
board, list the levels of government under which students live and categorize each role as federal,
state, or local government. Then show students the Unit 1 portion of the ***American Government:
Experience It!*** video, which profiles young people participating in local and state government to
make a difference in their communities.

> **L2 Differentiate** If students are not sure of the levels of government in the United States,
> use the list on the board or in the ***Essential Questions Journal*** and, starting with your
> community, explain each level, eliciting examples of each.

DAY 2

2. Introduce the Lesson Tell students that in this lesson they will discuss state constitutions,
including their origins and purposes, and why state governments exist. Begin by asking, **Why do
you think that there are state governments, with constitutions, when there is also a federal
government and Constitution?** *(Examples: To set up a state government, to regulate the safety and
welfare of citizens at the state level, to limit the power of the state government, and to pass and
execute laws on a more local level. Also, some state constitutions were written before there was a
national Constitution.)* Discuss the fact that each state has a unique geography and history. Ask
students to consider how their state's unique history, geography, and values might be expressed in
its constitution.

3. Complete the Activity Divide the class into pairs. Distribute copies of your state's constitution
to students. (You may obtain copies of the constitution from governmental offices, such as the
secretary of state, or online.) Then distribute ⬡**Activity 7.1,** *Analyzing Your State's Constitution,*
which lists the six basic principles of state constitutions. Tell students that they will work with a
partner to identify how their state constitution applies or addresses the six principles. After
students have completed the worksheets, have partners volunteer their examples and explain how
each one relates to the given principle.

> **L2 Differentiate** Before students begin the activity, list on the board the six principles on
> which each constitution is based. Define or explain each one that is on the board

4. Debrief Wrap up this activity by discussing federalism and the need for both state and federal
governments. Ask: **What activities can be carried out best by state and local governments?**
*(State governments can tailor laws and provisions specifically to the needs of people in that state
better than the federal government can, since the federal government must see to the needs of people
from all 50 states. Examples include zoning, public education, community policing, etc.)*

5. Assess Distribute ⬡**Assessment 7.1,** which asks students to identify which government level
should be responsible for which item and to state why that level should perform it. Discuss
students' ideas about the appropriateness of assigning the item to either state or federal
government. Explain to students which responsibilities are federal (national defense, foreign
relations), which are state (public schools, drivers' licenses, higher education, traffic laws), and
which are shared by state and federal governments.

EXTEND THE LESSON

L3 Differentiate Have students work in pairs to make a two-column chart comparing their state constitution to the United States Constitution. Ask them to share their completed charts, and then lead a class discussion examining reasons for the similarities and differences.

L2 Differentiate ELL Have visual learners or English Language Learners design a mural that illustrates all six principles of state constitutions. For "miscellaneous provisions," encourage students to study your state's constitution for ideas.

L4 Differentiate Have students write an essay that explains what is unique about their state and how their state's constitution addresses that uniqueness in ways that the United States Constitution does not.

UNIT 7

LESSON 2

The Structure and Functions of State and Local Governments

TEACHER INSTRUCTIONS

PURPOSE

To frame an answer to the 🌐 **Essential Question:** *What is the right balance of local, state, and federal government?,* students need to understand the structures, functions, responsibilities, and powers of state and local governments compared to those of the federal government.

LESSON GOALS

- Compare and contrast the structure, functions, and powers of state and local governments by completing a chart of government powers.
- Explain the need for both state and local governments.
- Create a poster to explain the roles, powers, and responsibilities of state and local governments.
- Explain the importance of the police power to state governments.

MATERIALS

- 🖸 **Online Student Edition** and copies of 🖸 **Background Note 7.2,** located at PearsonSuccessNet.com
- *Essential Questions Journal*
- Copies of 🖸 **Activity 7.2,** *Elements of State and Local Government,* located at PearsonSuccessNet.com
- Copies of 🖸 **Assessment 7.2,** located at PearsonSuccessNet.com

BEFORE CLASS

Distribute copies of 🖸 **Background Note 7.2.** For more in-depth information, refer students to the 🖸 **Online Student Edition,** Chapter 24, Sections 2 and 4, and Chapter 25, Sections 1 and 2. You may wish to have students read these materials before coming to class. You may also want students to complete the *Essential Questions Journal,* Unit 7 Warmup, p. 202; Chapter 24 Exploration, p. 204; and Chapter 25 Exploration, p. 211, before class.

L2 Differentiate Ask students to write down 3–5 main ideas from the Background Note, exchange them with a partner, and agree on three main points to share with the class. Write these points on the board and help students select those that create the most accurate summary.

L2 Differentiate Have students listen to the audio summary located at PearsonSuccessNet.com

TEACH

1. Introduce the Lesson Tell students that in this lesson they will discuss the structure and functions of state and local government. Explain that, like the federal government, all state constitutions established governments with three branches—executive, legislative, and judicial. One difference from the federal government is that a state government can only operate and make law within that particular state. Another important difference is that the United States Constitution reserves the police power to state legislatures rather than to Congress. Explain that governments take many different forms at the local level; some states are further divided into counties or townships, within which are towns, cities, and other communities. All authority of local governments originates with the state government. Explain which form of local government is used in your community and in other communities in your state.

2. Complete the Activity Divide the class into small groups. Then distribute ⊘**Activity 7.2,** *Elements of State and Local Governments.* Assign one of the following topics to each group: structure, functions, and powers of the state executive branch; structure, functions, and powers of the state legislative branch; structure, functions, and powers of the state judicial branch; structure, functions, and powers of your county/township government; and structure, functions, and powers of your town or municipal government. Tell students that they will work with group members using the information in their ⊘**Online Student Edition** and ⊘**Background Note 7.2** to complete one row of the worksheet. Students will then use their worksheets to present their review to the class and to record information from other groups' presentations. You may choose not to assign "county/township government" if it does not apply to your community.

> **L3 Differentiate** Ask students to use the Internet to fill in the worksheet based on their own state and local governments.

3. Debrief Wrap up ⊘**Activity 7.2** by discussing the need for both state and local governments. Ask: **Why do we need both state and local governments? What would it be like in our state and community if we had no local governments? Could the state government meet all its citizens' needs?** Ask students to identify areas where the roles of state and local governments differ or overlap and areas where they think either the state or local government might do a better job. For example, is there a need for a state police department? Should public education be managed at the local or state level? Encourage students to share their ideas about how powers and roles are distributed within their state.

4. Assess Distribute ⊘**Assessment 7.2,** which asks students to complete a graphic organizer and answer questions detailing the structure, functions, and other important features of state and local governments.

EXTEND THE LESSON

> **L3 Differentiate** Have students work in their groups to design and produce a poster using the information they learned about the structures and functions of state and local governments to answer the ⊛ **Essential Question:** *What is the right balance of local, state, and federal government?* For example, students could divide their poster into sections based on the importance they think each level has in their lives, with the most important level having the largest amount of space, and so on. Display finished posters in the classroom.

> **L2 Differentiate ELL** Have visual learners or English Language Learners complete a triple Venn diagram to compare and contrast the powers and roles of the federal, state, and local governments.

> **L4 Differentiate** Explain that since the New Deal of the 1930s, the U.S. Congress has taken on the police power in certain circumstances. Have students do research and write a short report on one example of a time when Congress exercised the police power.

TEACHER INSTRUCTIONS

PURPOSE

To frame an answer to the ❹ **Essential Question:** *What is the right balance of local, state, and federal government?*, students need to understand the essential services provided by state and local governments.

LESSON GOALS

- List and categorize services that students receive from state and local governments.
- Role-play to rank the importance of state and local services from different citizens' perspectives.
- Compare rankings of state services in order to understand the choices state and local governments face.

MATERIALS

- ❹ **Online Student Edition** and copies of ❹ **Background Note 7.3,** located at PearsonSuccessNet.com
- *Essential Questions Journal*
- Copies of ❹ **Activity 7.3,** *Rating State and Local Services,* located at PearsonSuccessNet.com
- Copies of ❹ **Assessment 7.3,** located at PearsonSuccessNet.com

BEFORE CLASS

Distribute copies of ❹ **Background Note 7.3.** For more in-depth information, refer students to the ❹ **Online Student Edition,** Chapter 25, Section 3. You may wish to have students read these materials before coming to class. You may also want students to complete the *Essential Questions Journal,* Unit 7 Warmup, p. 202, and Chapter 25 Exploration, p. 211, before class.

> **L2 Differentiate** Ask students to underline the main ideas of each paragraph in the Background Note. Have volunteers read aloud and explain their choices. (You may wish to limit this activity to paragraphs that you identify in advance.)

> **L2 Differentiate** Have students listen to the audio summary located at PearsonSuccessNet.com

TEACH

1. Introduce the Lesson Tell students that in this lesson they will discuss the types of services that are provided by state and local government. Begin by writing these headings on the board: **Education, Public Welfare, Public Safety, Public Health, Roads.** Have students suggest services they receive from state or local government, sort them under the appropriate category, and identify which level of government provides each service. Explain that most of these services are provided by state or local governments, not by the national government. Ask: **Why do you think these services are provided at the state or local level, and not by the national government?** *(Sample answer: State and local governments have better knowledge about how to meet the day-to-day needs of their citizens than the national government does.)*

2. Complete the Activity Divide the class into seven groups. Assign each group one of the following roles: student in the local high school, parent of three school-age children, police officer, taxi driver, carpenter, elderly resident, and worker who lives outside the community. Then rearrange students so that all roles are represented in each group and distribute ⊘ **Activity 7.3,** *Rating State and Local Services.* Tell students that they will complete the worksheet by role-playing people receiving various services provided by state and local governments. Then they will rank the various services and explain their reasoning based on the role they are playing.

> **L2 Differentiate** Before beginning, review the service categories on the worksheet and offer examples of each.

3. Debrief After students complete their individual role and group rankings, ask them to post their rankings around the room, as well as to explain their choice for their number-one ranking. Discuss any differences in the rankings from group to group. Then ask students to vote to create a class ranking. Discuss reasons for the class ranking.

> **L4 Differentiate** Have students write a journal entry explaining why they agree or disagree with the class ranking.

4. Assess Distribute ⊘ **Assessment 7.3,** which asks students to brainstorm a list of ten public services they receive, identify whether each is provided by the state or local government, and then rank them from most to least important.

EXTEND THE LESSON ▬▬▬▬

> **L3 Differentiate** Starting in 2008, the U.S. economy experienced a major downturn. Have students research to write a report on how this economic crisis affected services provided by their state. Reports should include what services were cut partially or completely, if any, and what services were maintained.

> **L2 Differentiate ELL** Have visual learners or English Language Learners gather images from old magazines or from the Internet to make a poster illustrating state and local services. For example, students might include images of their school, a police officer, and a highway construction crew. Tell students to label each image with the name of the service it represents and which level of government provides it in your state.

> **L4 Differentiate** Have students find a recent article that describes a difference of opinion on which level of government should provide a particular service or if the service, such as public schools, should be privatized. Ask students to summarize in a bulleted list the main arguments from each viewpoint. Then ask them to take a position on the issue and write a paragraph supporting their point of view.

State Revenue and Spending

TEACHER INSTRUCTIONS

PURPOSE

To frame an answer to the 🔂 **Essential Question:** *What is the right balance of local, state, and federal government?*, students need to understand the ways that state and local governments pay for their operations and the choices involved in raising, lowering, and changing taxes.

LESSON GOALS

- Categorize taxes as *progressive* or *regressive* by creating a two-column chart.
- Analyze graphs to understand the sources of state and local revenue and where the funds are spent.
- Evaluate state and local taxes based on Adam Smith's principles of sound taxation.

MATERIALS

- 🅐 **Online Student Edition** and copies of 🅐 **Background Notes 7.4 A** and **7.4 B,** located at PearsonSuccessNet.com
- *Essential Questions Journal*
- Copies of 🅐 **Activity 7.4,** *Evaluating Taxes,* located at PearsonSuccessNet.com
- Copies of 🅐 **Assessment 7.4,** located at PearsonSuccessNet.com

BEFORE CLASS

Distribute copies of 🅐 **Background Notes 7.4 A** and **7.4 B.** For more in-depth information, refer students to the 🅐 **Online Student Edition,** Chapter 25, Section 4. You may wish to have students read these materials before coming to class. You may also want students to complete the *Essential Questions Journal,* Unit 7 Warmup, p. 202, and Chapter 25 Exploration, p. 211, before class.

> **L2 Differentiate** Ask students to read aloud and define the boldfaced terms. Then have volunteers explain why these terms are important for understanding the Background Note.

> **L2 Differentiate** Have students listen to the audio summary located at PearsonSuccessNet.com

TEACH

1. Introduce the Lesson Tell students that in this lesson they will discuss how state and local governments raise and spend money. Explain that most state and local revenue is raised through taxes. Begin by creating a two-column chart on the board, with the headings **Progressive Taxes** and **Regressive Taxes.** Use 🅐 **Background Note 7.4 B** to review the meaning of these terms if they are unfamiliar to students. Ask students to name and categorize state and local taxes they pay or know about. Record their responses on the chart *(regressive: sales tax, property tax, excise tax, tax on movie tickets, tax on drivers' licenses; progressive: income tax).* Discuss why states levy different kinds of taxes. *(Any individual tax places a larger burden on some people than on others. A variety of taxes spreads the burden, making the tax system as a whole more fair.)* Point out that state and local governments do not rely solely on taxes for revenue; they also charge various fees and receive huge sums in grants and loans from the federal government.

L2 Differentiate Tell students to make a Venn diagram to compare and contrast features of progressive and regressive taxes, including examples of each.

2. Complete the Activity Distribute ✷**Activity 7.4,** *Evaluating Taxes.* Explain to students that Adam Smith was a Scottish economist whose 1776 book *The Wealth of Nations* proposed four tests for a sound tax system. Tell students that they will work with a partner to evaluate different types of state and local taxes based on Adam Smith's four criteria.

L2 Differentiate ELL Before beginning this portion of the lesson, have students read aloud each criterion and then restate it in their own words.

3. Debrief Discuss students' evaluations of the taxes. Ask students to raise their hands for "best" or "worst" as you name each tax on the worksheet, and record the vote on the board. Is there a general agreement on these designations? If so, have volunteers explain why they selected the taxes they did for the best and worst. If there is no consensus, discuss why there is so much difference of opinion on what is good tax policy. Ask students to explain what so many differences of opinion in your classroom might indicate about the difficulties of establishing tax policies in the larger world.

4. Assess Distribute ✷**Assessment 7.4,** which asks students to answer questions about taxes at the state level.

EXTEND THE LESSON

L3 Differentiate Have students research to find out how an individual citizen can seek changes to the tax law (such as joining interest groups, supporting political candidates, etc.) and report their findings to the class.

L2 Differentiate Have students create a concept web to show the various sources of state and local revenues, including the different types of taxes, borrowing, and other means of generating income.

L4 Differentiate Arrange students into groups of three or four. Have them research to find state and community government resources that provide information about specific revenue sources in your state, such as state or local budgets. Ask each group to create circle graphs illustrating (1) the sources of your state's revenues and (2) how those revenues are distributed and spent in your community. Tell students to include a summary explaining each graph.

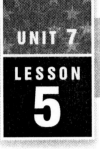

TEACHER INSTRUCTIONS

PURPOSE

To frame an answer to the ✦ **Essential Question:** *What is the right balance of local, state, and federal government?,* students need to understand how citizens can participate in the lawmaking process directly through initiative and referendum.

LESSON GOALS

- Explain the purpose of the initiative and referendum.
- Research and answer questions about a specific initiative or state constitutional amendment and share answers in a class discussion.

MATERIALS

- ⊘ **Online Student Edition** and copies of ⊘ **Background Note 7.5,** located at PearsonSuccessNet.com
- *Essential Questions Journal*
- Copies of ⊘ **Activity 7.5,** *Civic Participation in Lawmaking,* located at PearsonSuccessNet.com
- Copies of ⊘ **Assessment 7.5,** located at PearsonSuccessNet.com

BEFORE CLASS

Distribute copies of ⊘ **Background Note 7.5.** For more in-depth information, refer students to the ⊘ **Online Student Edition,** Chapter 24, Sections 1 and 2. You may wish to have students read these materials before coming to class. You may also want students to complete the *Essential Questions Journal,* Unit 7 Warmup, p. 202, and Chapter 24 Exploration, p. 204, before class.

> **L2 Differentiate** Instead of students reading the Background Note on their own, have volunteers take turns reading portions aloud in class. After each portion is read, have a volunteer other than the reader summarize the information.

> **L2 Differentiate** Have students listen to the audio summary located at PearsonSuccessNet.com

TEACH

1. Introduce the Lesson Tell students that in this lesson they will discuss how legislation is made by citizens at the state level. Most laws are passed by state legislatures, where they are introduced by legislators, but they may come from agencies, local governments, interest groups, or the public. In addition, in many states citizens may directly propose legislation through the *initiative.* Citizens may also accept or reject ballot questions through the *referendum.* Write the terms *referendum* and *initiative* on the board, and have volunteers define each term. Then, as a class, complete a flowchart to outline each process. Explain that these crucial tools of direct democracy were not always available to citizens in the United States, but grew out of reform movements of the nineteenth and early twentieth centuries that sought to increase popular sovereignty. Explain that this form of lawmaking takes place only at a state level, not at the federal level.

2. Complete the Activity Distribute ⦿ **Activity 7.5,** *Civic Participation in Lawmaking.* Tell students that they will research to identify and summarize a specific initiative or constitutional amendment in their own or another state. You may wish to assign this research as homework.

> **L2 Differentiate** If your state does not allow the initiative, give students examples of states that do.

3. Debrief Have students report on the lawmaking process in the state, the topic of the legislation they researched, and whether or not the law passed. Based on students' findings, discuss the nature of citizen-sponsored legislation—what types of laws citizens usually try to pass and how successful these efforts are.

4. Assess Distribute ⦿ **Assessment 7.5,** which asks students to complete a Venn diagram to compare and contrast features of the initiative and referendum and to answer questions about civic participation in lawmaking.

EXTEND THE LESSON

L3 Differentiate Have students research to investigate the arguments for and against the use of the referendum and initiative. Have students use their research to engage in a classroom debate.

L2 Differentiate Ask students to draw a concept web titled "Initiatives, Referenda, and Constitutional Amendments" using the information they learned in this lesson.

L4 Differentiate Have students research the concept and status of the drive to create an initiative process for the federal government and write an essay that explains their findings and discusses whether they believe that the initiative and referendum should be used at the national level.

TEACHER INSTRUCTIONS

PURPOSE

To frame an answer to the ❓ **Essential Question:** *What is the right balance of local, state, and federal government?,* students will learn how to be an active participant in the decision-making process of local government.

LESSON GOALS

- Analyze source material to help make an informed decision on local government issues.
- Apply students' understandings of local government to real-life situations.

MATERIALS

- ⊘ **Online Interactive Decision Making,** located at PearsonSuccessNet.com
- *Essential Questions Journal*

BEFORE CLASS

Refer students to the ⊘ **Online Student Edition** Chapter 24 and Chapter 25. You may wish to have students read this material before coming to class. You may also want students to complete the *Essential Questions Journal,* Chapter 24 Exploration, pp. 204–208, and Chapter 25 Exploration, pp. 211–214, before class if they have not already done so.

TEACH

1. Introduce the Lesson Write the following headings on the board: **Executive, Legislative,** and **Judicial.** Based on their reading in their textbooks, have students list at least three facts under each heading. Then discuss the responsibilities of state and local governments, the way they raise revenue, and the various services that they provide. Then explain how the three branches of government function specifically in their own states as well as the unique characteristics of their local communities.

2. Complete the Activity Have students complete the online activity in class or assign it as homework. (NOTE: *If you decide to give this as a homework assignment, conduct the Debrief at the beginning of class and then continue with the next day's lesson plan described on the following page.*)

3. Debrief Once students have completed the online interactivity, ask them to compare their experiences. What information or source did they find influenced their vote? Why is it necessary to learn more about an issue on a ballot before voting on it? How can they affect change in their community?

4. Assess Have students select one of the issues addressed in the activity and conduct research to find out how it would be addressed according to the policies and procedures regulating their local government. You may wish to have students share these conclusions in class.

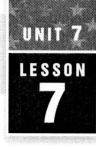

Participating in State and Local Government

TEACHER INSTRUCTIONS

PURPOSE

To frame an answer to the ✪ **Essential Question:** *What is the right balance of local, state, and federal government?*, students will conduct a Local Government simulation in which they apply the information learned throughout this unit to determine what action could be taken at the local and state levels of government to achieve community goals.

LESSON GOALS

- Apply knowledge about the different roles of state and local government and issues of government budgets by analyzing and making recommendations for a local budget.
- Explain how citizens involve the various levels of government to address a problem.
- Debate alternative solutions to a state and local issue to learn ways citizens can affect or participate in the lawmaking process.
- Evaluate and synthesize information, make decisions, and demonstrate reasoned judgment.

MATERIALS

- ⊘ **Online Student Edition,** located at PearsonSuccessNet.com
- **State/Local 7.a—Town of Willow Heights Map** Map offering a frame of reference for understanding the scenario. Map shows political boundaries and geographic features of the fictional town of Willow Heights and the township of Oakhill in Acheson County. Students will use this map to assist in their decision making.

  State/Local 7.b:—Town Annual Budget Budget sheet providing the annual budget information for Willow Heights, including the projected budget deficit and proposed cuts.

  State/Local 7.c:—Acheson County Facts Fact card providing background information on the town of Willow Heights to inform student decisions about policy.

  State/Local 7.d:—SunGold Brochure Corporate marketing brochure explaining the benefits of SunGold Innovations' proposed new facility.

  State/Local 7.e:—*Willow Heights Today* News Story News report describing a current protest against SunGold in another community.

- Copies of ⊘ **Activity 7.7,** *Five Types of State Government Involvement,* located at PearsonSuccessNet.com

BEFORE CLASS

Post the map of Willow Heights **(State/Local 7.a)**, the town budget sheet **(State/Local 7.b)**, and the county fact sheet **(State/Local 7.c).** You may also wish to copy and distribute the budget and fact sheets to each student. Have students review the map and budget before class.

TEACH

1. Introduce the Lesson Explain to students that this activity will give them insight and understanding into how decisions are made in local government and how citizens can participate in lawmaking at the state level to resolve issues. Tell students that they will be role-playing residents of the fictional town Willow Heights, which is experiencing a budget crisis and must consider different solutions to solve it. Discuss the map and budget and answer students' questions about the activity scenario.

> **L2 Differentiate ELL** Suggest that students list any words on the map or budget that they do not understand. After they have looked the words up in a dictionary, have them look back at the budget with their definitions close at hand.

> **L4 Differentiate** Have students research any budget cuts that might recently have been made in their own community or state. Ask students to find out how much the deficit was and what was cut to reduce spending and report this information to the class.

DAY 1

1. Review the Town Budget As a class, hold a Willow Heights town council meeting to review the budget and to discuss the deficit and how to balance the budget. You may act as moderator, or appoint a student volunteer. Based on the information in the budget and the profile of Willow Heights on the fact card, discuss the town's deficit. Point out that it is almost $5 million. As voters of Willow Heights, have students make arguments for some specific cuts that they would make from the list of Proposals/Estimated Savings and vote to select some combination that will balance the budget. Discuss with students how they made their selections and, if they are unhappy with the result, ask them to explain their own ideas. Which groups in the town will be most affected by the cuts? Tell students that most communities face similar budget challenges each year.

2. Introduce SunGold Tell students that a company called SunGold Innovations has recently introduced a proposal to build a new research facility in Willow Heights. On the map of Willow Heights **(State/Local 7.a)** show students where SunGold is proposing to build and which major roads and waterways might be affected by the new facility.

3. Write Recommendations Break the class into five groups. Explain that each group will play the role of a citizen's group that has volunteered to report on the benefits and drawbacks of having SunGold build a new facility in town. Write on the board: **Will SunGold be the solution to Willow Heights' budget crisis?** Each group will answer this question by discussing the issues surrounding the new facility and working together to write a summary of their recommendation to the town. Have each group study **State/Local 7.d** and **7.e** at stations, and rotate groups through each station as they work. Summaries should be based on students' review of the lesson materials, keeping in mind the current budget pressures, environmental issues, economic growth versus quality of life, and so on. You may choose to identify these areas of study and assign them to different groups. *(Note: You may wish to assign students the following roles within their citizen groups: librarian, police officer, senior citizen, property owner whose property abuts the proposed SunGold site, member of the "Keep Open Spaces in Willow Heights" committee, farmer.)*

> **L2 Differentiate** Suggest that students make a Pro/Con list drawn from the information in the materials, the town meeting budget vote, and their own ideas and prior knowledge. They can use the Pro/Con list to help them formulate their personal recommendation to their group.

4. Discuss and Vote Have each group read its recommendation, which should include reasons that support its viewpoints, to the entire class in a town council meeting on the SunGold issue. When each group has reported, allow individuals to express further ideas or arguments for or against SunGold's proposal. Then have students raise their hands to vote "Yes" or "No" on accepting SunGold's proposal, and tally the vote on the board. Discuss with students the outcome of the vote and how, as citizens, they feel about the fairness of the process. Do they think that voters made the best decision for the town?

DAY 2

1. Announce SunGold's Decision Have students assemble as the whole-class town meeting. Then announce (or have the student moderator announce) that SunGold has decided not to build in Willow Heights, but to build outside the town, further west on Payton Road and the Clearwater River, in Oakhill Township. Point out the general location of the planned site on the map **(State/Local 7.a)**. Explain that in this location, Willow Heights will not benefit from additional tax revenue or the new stadium, although citizens will have access to some of the new jobs. Most significantly, Willow Heights will experience all the drawbacks—light and air pollution, traffic congestion, and road wear. Refer students to the article in *Willow Heights Today* **(State/Local 7.e)** about the problems caused by SunGold's Jasperville facility.

2. Research a Solution at the State Level Have students re-form in their groups from Day 1. Tell them that they are again serving Willow Heights by investigating how a town in their state might involve the state government to solve the problem with SunGold. Distribute at least one copy of ⊘**Activity 7.7**, *Five Types of State Government Involvement,* to each group. Tell students that voters have decided to require SunGold to pay impact fees to Willow Heights to compensate the town for any air, noise, light, or water pollution and for necessary roadway improvements to accommodate new traffic. SunGold has refused. Have students do research in their online textbook, in the library, or on the Internet to find out about the different processes the town could follow at the state level to force SunGold to pay impact fees. *(Note: You may wish to assign this research for homework.)*

> **L2 Differentiate** Explain that new developments, like the SunGold facility or housing developments, can stress local services and infrastructure. Explain that an *impact fee* is a charge on new construction or development to pay for the costs of necessary improvements to roads, utilities, and schools.

3. Discuss By the end of the class period, each group should have discussed their findings for each process on **Activity 7.7** and come to a decision about which process they will recommend to the town. Have students finalize their decision and work to create a recommendation to present to Willow Heights' voters at the next town council meeting, tomorrow. For example, one group may decide to recommend that the town work to get an initiative on the next state election ballot that will make impact fees legal, if they are not already, in your state. If the fees are already legal in your state, students may find that the best process is to file in local or state courts for an injunction to stop the construction. Make sure students keep in mind that they want to achieve the best and most efficient outcome for the town, within what is possible in your state, and that their summaries should include the basic steps the town will need to follow.

DAY 3

1. Debrief Have groups report on which process at the state level they selected. If there is more than one choice, have groups with unique processes read their summaries aloud so that each recommended choice is presented. Then have the "voters" (the class) vote by a show of hands to select the process that they want to follow, keeping in mind all recommendations of the groups and the information in the presentations. When voting is complete, announce the winning process. Ask students to write a paragraph that explains why they did or did not support it.

2. Assess Have students answer the **Essential Question:** *What is the right balance of local, state, and federal government?* in their *Essential Questions Journal.* You may also use one of the following formats:

> **Assessment option 1: Present answer in an essay**
> **Assessment option 2: Present answer in a multimedia format**
> **Assessment option 3: Present answer in a visual format**

3. Conclude Point out that, through this Local Government simulation, students should have gained a better understanding of how citizens make decisions at the local level, how accessible the state legislative process is to citizens, and what the balance is between state and local governments. Ask: **Do you feel that your state or local government would have been effective in helping Willow Heights? Why or why not?**

EXTEND THE LESSON

L3 Differentiate Have students research and write a report on an actual case in your community or state where a development project was proposed that faced significant debate. Students should explain the main issues of the case and identify the levels, branches, and agencies of government that were involved; the main views of both sides; and the outcome.

L2 Differentiate Have students take the information their group recorded in **Activity 7.7** and reformat it into a graphic organizer about how new law can be made in your state.

L4 Differentiate Instruct students to determine and report on how the citizens of Willow Heights might have involved the federal government, as well as the state government, in helping to resolve their issue with SunGold. For example, students might investigate whether or not the Environmental Protection Agency or another federal regulatory agency might have stepped in and what that agency might have accomplished.

Rubric for Assessing a Role Play

Grading Criteria	Excellent	Acceptable	Minimal	Unacceptable
Content	Displays thorough knowledge of topic; includes all main facts; no errors in accuracy.	Displays adequate knowledge of topic; includes most main facts; few errors in accuracy.	Displays superficial knowledge of topic; omits several main facts; several errors in accuracy.	Displays misunderstanding of topic; omits most main facts; many errors in accuracy.
Organization	Well organized; roles come together into a coherent whole; dialogue supports central theme.	Mostly well organized; most action and dialogue support central theme.	Organization uneven; some action and dialogue irrelevant to theme.	Disorganized; much of the action and dialogue are off theme.
Creativity	Very original presentation; includes exceptionally clever elements; captures and holds audience attention throughout.	Some originality apparent; captures and holds audience attention through most of performance.	Little originality apparent; loses audience attention during performance.	Displays little or no creative effort; fails to capture audience attention.
Costumes and Props	Very creatively chosen or made; all are appropriate to content; greatly enhance interest in and understanding of performance.	Mostly creatively chosen or made; most are appropriate to content; most contribute to interest in and understanding of performance.	Little creative effort apparent in choice or creation; some are inappropriate to content; contribute little to interest in or understanding of performance.	Almost no effort apparent in choice or creation; most are inappropriate to content; make no significant contribution to interest in or understanding of performance.
Performance	Well rehearsed; smooth flow of action with no lapses; speaking roles performed with clear articulation and confidence.	Displays some evidence of practice; action generally flows smoothly with few lapses; most speeches are clearly articulated.	Displays little evidence of practice; action jerky with several lapses; several speeches not clearly articulated.	No practice evident; many lapses in action; most speeches not clearly articulated.

Rubric for Assessing an Oral Presentation

Grading Criteria	Excellent	Acceptable	Minimal	Unacceptable
Preparation	Gathers information from many reputable sources; prepares thorough and helpful notes (or speaks clearly from memory); creates attractive visual aids to support the presentation.	Gathers information from varied and appropriate sources; prepares notes or visual aids to use during presentation.	Gathers minimal information from one or two sources; the sources may or may not be appropriate or sufficient; does not prepare many notes or visual aids.	Gathers limited information from one easy-to-find source; may not be able to complete task because of lack of preparation.
Content	Abundance of material clearly relates to the topic; points are interesting and clear; presentation has coherent thesis.	Has adequate information about the topic; makes good points; has a clear thesis.	Not enough adequate or total content provided; some information may not be relevant; thesis is simple or unclear.	Information included has little connection to the topic; no explicit or acceptable thesis is provided.
Organization	Information is well organized and logically ordered; argument is easy to follow; conclusion is clear.	Most information is presented in a logical order; argument is generally clear and easy to follow.	Ideas are loosely connected; organization and flow are choppy and somewhat difficult to follow.	Seemingly random or unconnected information is presented; organization has not been thought through.
Speaking Skills	Speaker is engaging, poised, and confident during the presentation; speaks clearly, naturally, and fluently.	Speaker is mostly engaging during the presentation; speaks clearly and fluently during most of the presentation.	Speaker is not very engaging; speech is wooden, enunciation is not always clear; lots of "er" or "um," no eye contact, etc.	Speaker appears uninterested, afraid, or unfocused during presentation; is difficult to understand.

Rubric for Assessing a Debate

Grading Criteria	Excellent	Acceptable	Minimal	Unacceptable
Preparation	Student uses several reliable sources to research topic; prepares thorough notes outlining arguments on both sides of the issue.	Student uses reliable sources to research topic; prepares thorough notes outlining one side of the issue.	Student uses few or unreliable sources to research topic; notes are lacking in content and may be too disorganized to use.	Student does not use sources to research the topic; student does not prepare notes.
Procedure	During the debate, the student speaks clearly and loudly at appropriate times, listens carefully to others' arguments, and responds with strong evidence.	Student generally speaks clearly and loudly; listens to others' arguments and responds appropriately.	Student speaks softly or unclearly; recites only "prepared" remarks rather than responding to others.	Student does not participate or makes inappropriate remarks.
Content	Arguments, examples, and evidence are accurate, relevant, and very effective in proving or rebutting a point.	Arguments, examples, and evidence are accurate, relevant, and generally effective in proving or rebutting a point.	Arguments, examples, or evidence may be inaccurate at times, irrelevant, or ineffective.	Arguments, examples, and evidence are ineffective, inaccurate, and irrelevant.

Rubric for Assessing Performance of an Entire Group

Grading Criteria	Excellent	Acceptable	Minimal	Unacceptable
Participation	All team members make important contributions toward goals. Team makes excellent use of members' skills and talents.	All team members participate; team makes use of members' skills and talents.	Some team members do not participate or participate only minimally.	A few team members do all the work.
Teamwork	Team members demonstrate enthusiasm, work together effectively, and solve problems without outside help.	Team members generally work together effectively and attempt to solve problems without outside help.	Team members usually work as if working alone, with little communication. Team requires outside help to solve problems.	Team members are unable to work together.
Accuracy	All team members complete assignments accurately.	Most team members complete assignments accurately; team works together to support members who may not understand their assignments.	Some team members do not complete assignments; team is unable to help members who submit inaccurate assignments, or different members redo assignment.	Some team members do not complete assignments.
Presentation or Final Product	Exceeds assignment criteria; is organized and creative.	Meets all and exceeds some assignment criteria; is organized and creative.	Meets some assignment criteria; may be disorganized or lack creativity.	Meets few or no assignment criteria; shows lack of preparation.

Rubric for Assessing a Graph, Chart, or Table

Grading Criteria	Excellent	Acceptable	Minimal	Unacceptable
Content	Includes the most pertinent information. Information is complete, accurate, and sources are cited where appropriate.	Meets assignment criteria; few or no inaccuracies.	Partially fulfills assignment criteria; information may be partially inaccurate or irrelevant.	Does not meet the assignment criteria; information is inaccurate or irrelevant.
Graph, Chart, or Table Elements	Title and labels are clear, concise, and accurate; all required elements are included.	Title and labels are clear and accurate; all required elements are included.	Title is included; some labels are missing; labels are inaccurate; most required elements are included.	Does not include required elements; information is inaccurate.
Visual Appeal	Clean and neat; labels are easy to read; color enhances effectiveness; may use creative graphics related to the content.	Clean and neat; labels are easy to read; color enhances effectiveness.	Parts of graph, chart, or table are difficult to read; color adds little value.	Graph, chart, or table is difficult to read; color adds no value.
Mechanics	Proper format is used; information is displayed precisely; sources are cited where appropriate; spelling and grammar are accurate.	Proper format is used; information is displayed accurately; sources are cited where appropriate; few or no errors in spelling and grammar.	Information is displayed with some minor errors in format or accuracy; source citations may be missing.	Improper format is used; information is displayed inaccurately.

Rubric for Assessing a Writing Assignment

Grading Criteria	Excellent	Acceptable	Minimal	Unacceptable
Purpose	Purpose of writing is clear and reflects assignment.	Purpose of writing is discernable and reflects assignment.	Purpose of writing may be unclear or partly off topic.	Purpose of writing is unclear or off topic.
Content	Content is appropriate to assignment; introduction engages reader; ideas are well developed with substantial detail and evidence; conclusion is strongly related to content.	Content is mostly appropriate to assignment; introduction makes sense; ideas are developed and elaborated with detail and evidence; conclusion makes sense with content.	Some content may be irrelevant to the assignment; introduction is unclear; ideas are partially developed and minimally supported; conclusion does not seem to be drawn from content.	Content does not meet assignment criteria; no introduction; ideas are not developed or supported; no conclusion is provided.
Organization	Structure is clear and appropriate to writing type; includes clear introduction, well-developed body, and clear conclusion; writing is organized logically into paragraphs and sentences.	Structure is generally clear and appropriate to writing type; includes introduction, body, and conclusion; writing is organized into paragraphs and sentences.	Structure may be partially unclear, inappropriate, or lacking; introduction or conclusion is lacking or minimal; organization of paragraphs or construction of sentences is flawed.	Structure is largely unclear, inappropriate, or lacking; introduction or conclusion is missing; significant flaws in organization of paragraphs or construction of sentences.
Mechanics	Flawless spelling, punctuation, and grammar; varied sentence structure.	Minor spelling, punctuation, or grammar errors; somewhat varied sentence structure.	Careless spelling, punctuation, or grammar errors; repetitive sentence structure.	Significant spelling, punctuation, or grammar errors; poor sentence structure.

Rubric for Assessing Individual Performance in a Group

Grading Criteria	Excellent	Acceptable	Minimal	Unacceptable
Participation	Willingly contributes creative ideas; listens attentively to others' ideas; considers all views; completes all assignments on time.	Contributes several good ideas; listens to others' ideas; usually considers all views; completes assignments on time.	Participates only by agreeing with others' ideas; contributes no original ideas; sometimes listens to others' ideas; only considers some views; completes some assignments late.	Makes few or irrelevant contributions; is inattentive; does not complete assignments.
Teamwork	Works cooperatively with all group members; elicits contributions from other group members; provides constructive feedback to other group members; completes all aspects of assigned role.	Works well with most group members; usually elicits contributions from other group members; provides some feedback to other group members; actively works in assigned role.	Has difficulty working cooperatively; sometimes elicits contributions from other group members; provides minimal feedback to other group members; partially fulfills assigned role.	Allows other group members to do most of the work; provides no feedback to other group members; does not work in assigned role.
Presentation of Ideas or Project	Exceeds assignment criteria; is organized and creative; participates fully in presentation.	Fulfills assignment criteria; participates somewhat in presentation.	Meets some assignment criteria; participates minimally in presentation.	Does not meet assignment criteria; does not participate in presentation.

Rubric for Assessing a Political Cartoon

Grading Criteria	Excellent	Acceptable	Minimal	Unacceptable
Message	Key issue and cartoonist's position are clearly identifiable.	Key issue and cartoonist's position are identifiable.	Key issue is identifiable; cartoonist's position may be unclear.	Key issue and cartoonist's position are unclear.
Visual Presentation and Creativity	Cartoon is neat and clean; color and creative graphics are used exceptionally well; captions are readable.	Cartoon is neat and clean; color and creative graphics are used; captions are readable.	Cartoon is somewhat neat; some color and creative graphics are used; captions are included.	Cartoon is messy; color and graphics are lacking; captions are omitted or unreadable.
Content	Cartoon clearly conveys an understanding of the issue; excellent use of appropriate symbolism; title is clear, clever, and relevant to topic.	Cartoon conveys understanding of the issue; uses appropriate symbolism; title is clear and relevant to topic.	Cartoon conveys a limited understanding of the issue; attempts to use symbolism; title is unclear or irrelevant to topic.	Cartoon conveys little or no understanding of the issue; does not use symbolism; title is missing.